Writing the Radical Memoir

Writing the Radical Memoir

A Theoretical and Craft-based Approach

Paul Williams and Shelley Davidow

BLOOMSBURY ACADEMIC
LONDON • NEW YORK • OXFORD • NEW DELHI • SYDNEY

BLOOMSBURY ACADEMIC
Bloomsbury Publishing Plc
50 Bedford Square, London, WC1B 3DP, UK
1385 Broadway, New York, NY 10018, USA
29 Earlsfort Terrace, Dublin 2, Ireland

BLOOMSBURY, BLOOMSBURY ACADEMIC and the Diana logo
are trademarks of Bloomsbury Publishing Plc

First published in Great Britain 2023

Cover design by Jess Stevens
Cover image © Plateresca/ Getty Images

A catalogue record for this book is available from the British Library.

A catalog record for this book is available from the Library of Congress.

ISBN: HB: 978-1-3502-7220-0
         PB: 978-1-3502-7221-7
       ePDF: 978-1-3502-7222-4
      eBook: 978-1-3502-7223-1

Typeset by Integra Software Services Pvt. Ltd.

To find out more about our authors and books visit www.bloomsbury.com
and sign up for our newsletters.

For Annie of Annie's Books in Peregian – holder of stories – with love P & S

Contents

Illustrations

About the authors

Paul Williams is Senior Lecturer in Creative Writing and Deputy Head of Research in the School of Business and Creative Industries at the University of the Sunshine Coast, Australia. He has published prize-winning fiction, young adult novels, memoir, non-fiction and short stories, a series of crime novels, and textbooks on creative writing including *Novel Ideas: Writing Innovative Fiction* (2019) and *Playing with Words: An Introduction to Creative Writing Craft* (2016), co-authored with Shelley Davidow. www.paulwilliamsauthor.com

Shelley Davidow is Senior Lecturer in the School of Education at the University of the Sunshine Coast, Australia. An international author of forty-six books, her recent titles include the memoirs *Runaways* (2022), *Shadow Sisters* (2018), *Whisperings in the Blood* (2016) and the creative writing textbook *Playing with Words: An Introduction to Creative Writing Craft* co-authored with Paul Williams. www.shelleydavidow.com

Introduction: What is radical memoir?

What is memoir, if not a raging against the dying of the light? We throw our voices out into the darkness in the hope that we will be heard by others. We hope that by being heard, we are made valid, our lives are worthy, that we matter somehow.

This book is a memoir too. It is in the form of a textbook. Or a handbook. Or an academic book. But it's also a literary legacy, our own way of raging against the dying of the light.

In this book, we offer readers our combined decades of writing knowledge, experience and insight in the hope that you, the reader/writer, might be able to avoid some of the pitfalls of writing memoir, and in the hope that what we've created inspires you to write your life onto the page and make your story into a compelling literary narrative.

Writing the Radical Memoir is a journey into unchartered territory, using the maps of those who have gone before.

We aren't the first and we won't be the last to attempt to hold our stories to the light and invite others into our lived experiences. Two hundred years ago, the British Romantics, obsessed with love and mortality and the finiteness of things, sought immortality through their words. Many of them died young. John Keats wrote 'Ode on a Grecian Urn' (Keats 1819: 638) in order to capture the transience of human experience in art. In that poem, he describes images that have been painted on an urn by some Ancient Greek artist, and he meditates on a lover who is pursuing his beloved and a scene in which a precious moment is frozen in time. Keats muses about how the lovers' young love will be forever preserved, this scene immortalized through art, on the urn:

> When old age shall this generation waste,
> Thou shalt remain, in midst of other woe
> Than ours, a friend to man, to whom thou say'st,
> 'Beauty is truth, truth beauty, – that is all
> Ye know on earth, and all ye need to know.'

(Keats 1819: 638)

The Grecian urn reveals the artist's craving to preserve a story of lives lived, just as Keats's poem about that urn is his attempt to immortalize the story on the side of the urn, and his own life. He is moved by those depicted on the urn – a physical record of the passing of individuals, of their hopes and dreams and moments of joy. Perhaps fearing his own near end (he died aged twenty-six, of tuberculosis), Keats wrote this poem to preserve, to cherish. And he succeeded. More than 200 years after he died, we feel for the young man who wrote that poem, and for the late artist before him who carved the lovers onto the side of the urn. Although the poem is not a memoir in the way we think of memoir, it is perhaps a radical memoir, a conscious preservation in words, of lived experiences for future generations.

Percy Shelley, another Romantic poet, wrote 'Ozymandias' (1818) about the attempts of ancient kings to make themselves immortal. In the poem he derides the great King Ramos the Third for attempting to write his memory into history for ever, as a vast statue in the desert inspiring fear, yet ending up after thousands of years as a colossal wreck – but still there, mind you. The statue's 'vast and trunkless legs of stone stand in the desert' (Shelley 1818: 24). Like Keats, Percy Shelley himself died young but, miraculously, his poem gives him an existence hundreds of years beyond his own lifetime – which is surely what he wanted.

Memoir, defined as the telling of our own personal narratives in some form or another, has been around since the beginning of human consciousness. Cave paintings by the San people in Southern Africa, for example, record the exploits of people tens of thousands of years ago. The Valley of the Kings in Egypt could be seen as a colossal collective memoir. Stories in hieroglyphics, statues and pyramids and sarcophagi attempt to preserve human stories, both factual and mythical, for eternity. So much of what we write is to preserve, to capture the lived experience of an individual. Every memoir is to some degree an attempt to reach out to those who may never know us in the present and say, *I lived this, let me live again through your knowing. I'm born again when you bring me to life in your imagination.*

People write memoir for a variety of reasons. What 'good' memoir does is connect us to one another through our stories and our humanity. The more authentic, the more skilled, the more evocative the writing, just like the most potent of paintings or visual images, the more lasting the impression.

Words matter as the proxy for experiences and thoughts in memoir. Since time began humans have told their stories first via images on the walls of caves and, later, carved into stone via symbols; they have passed personal and collective narratives on via oral histories and finally in written texts. Memoir writers are word-artists, and their tools matter as much as the tools of skilled painters. We hope to give you, the reader/writer, a set of those tools.

As writers, we throw our words into the future, and if, like the romantic poets, the words are crafted skilfully, they may last. Our stories may continue, and we may live on through our words. Walt Whitman, the nineteenth-century American poet, put it this way:

> The question, O me! so sad, recurring – What good amid these, O me, O life?
> Answer.
> That you are here – that life exists and identity,
> That the powerful play goes on, and you may contribute a verse.
> (Whitman 1982: 410)

May this book help you contribute that verse …

The shortest memoir ever written

Recently, we were walking along the wide expanse of Alexandra Bay in Noosa, Australia, on a stretch of several kilometres of white beach, looking out at a timeless blue sea one summer afternoon at low tide. At the end of a set of footprints in the sand, we found the words *I was here.*

What is this desire to leave a mark, to make our presence felt? Why does it matter that we're acknowledged, that we are seen, heard, that our stories don't fall on deaf ears? According to a paramedic who is often with people as they die, this is one of the primary concerns of those who know their end is near: *will you remember me?*

> The second pattern I observe is the need for remembrance. (Whether it was to be remembered in my thoughts or their loved ones', they needed to feel that they would be living on. There's a need for immortality within the hearts and thoughts of their loved ones, myself, my crew, or anyone around.) Countless times, I have had a patient look me in the eyes and say, 'Will you remember me?' The final pattern I observe always touched me the deepest, to the soul. The dying need to know that their life had meaning. They need to know that they did not waste their life on meaningless tasks.
>
> (O'Reilly 2014: np)

From the earliest cave paintings to the simple marks that lovers leave on trees, we're telling the stories of our lives, so that those who come after might feel, be moved or interested or connected to the people we are and to the memories and stories that we leave behind.

Radical memoir

The word 'radical' has various connotations, positive and negative. Radical means 'fundamental', 'going to the root of things', 'extreme', 'thoroughgoing', 'drastic', 'very new and different from the usual or ordinary'. We often associate a radical with a troublemaker, an extremist, a fanatic who goes to excess. But, originally, 'radical' simply meant getting to the centre or heart of something, from the Latin *radicalis,* meaning root. We have chosen to call this book *Writing the Radical Memoir* in order to get to the root of memoir, but also to push the idea of memoir to the limit. We question simplistic notions of what memoir is and hope to create something new and different. This book therefore offers a dynamic investigation of the theory and practice of memoir writing, challenging conventional assumptions about how we tell the truth about ourselves. We would like to radically question the assumptions regarding writing memoir. This book is underpinned by theory and practice by experienced writers/teachers and contains innovative exercises that stimulate quality creative practice. We incorporate poststructuralist and postmodern theories of the self from Barthes, Lacan, Derrida and contemporary memoir writers, and challenge writers to understand how language is used and how the 'self' is constructed. But we also push against such theory because we are, first and foremost, artists of words, creative writers – and the spaces we inhabit are messy and non-linear and not pre-prescribed.

Whilst our studios are not necessarily flecked with paint and spills and abandoned canvasses full of potential but lacking in direction, our minds, our computer files and thousands of unpublished pages are the equivalent. We aim to support writers to be messy, to be liberated from the structures – even good and often useful ones – that may bury the artist's impulse. In this book, we will push the envelope.

A radical memoir then is a uniquely individual and authentic recollection and reconstruction of a life through words, a pastiche of psycho-spiritual-emotional experiences that have made us who we are. A radical memoir does not provide a simple translation of facts or history into words: it is rather a construct of a provisional self, a selective set of memories, recalled and re-arranged to create a story that employs a range of craft-based skills and narrative elements. Neuroscience tells us that all remembering is a recreating. Memoir is a product of imagination as much as fiction is and involves a significant amount of unwriting, erasing, playing, unravelling, deconstruction and re-creating, using all the skills of fiction-writing to make a compelling story. As memoir writers, we aim to create narratives that are emotionally true to our experience of the world. The tools that may help are many and the pathway is uneven, challenging, exhilarating and unpredictable.

Each chapter of this book is underpinned by a range of theories about writing memoir, autobiography and life writing: we draw on a wide array of literary examples as well as from the publications, teaching and writing experiences of the two authors, and offer a range of practical, performative exercises that can be used in creative writing workshops for the general public, in university courses on memoir, for individual memoir writers and potentially for anyone interested in life-writing as a journey of self-development.

Writing the Radical Memoir arose out of the many writing workshops we have conducted across decades and continents – Africa, the Middle East, Europe, North America, Oceania. The material emerges from years of teaching writing both to the general public and to creative writing students at universities. The material in this book has been tested in Master of Creative Writing classes, undergraduate courses in writing creative non-fiction at various universities, as well as in community workshops that both authors have run over decades.

We hope to encourage a broad and dynamic awareness of the territory of memoir writing, and we draw on classes and approaches that have been run in diverse settings, with people of all ages from everywhere.

Defining the genre: What is memoir?

Paul

As a child I used to browse through all the different sections of bookstores and libraries just to absorb the feeling of the thousands of books, and I remember marvelling at the way they were categorized. Fiction was my favourite section – a swathe of stories all untrue, made up, from sci-fi to crime to literary fiction. Stories. I would loiter in this section. I lived in a fantasy world, in my imagination. I found non-fiction, the news, politics and science boring. Although I could not articulate why, I knew that for me fiction and storytelling got to the heart of the matter, to the mythical roots or distilled essence of things. My father was different. He liked facts, figures, history. 'Why would anyone want to read things that are not true?' he would ask me. In the bookstores and libraries that we frequented, he would browse the Non-Fiction section, the 'true' section where everything written about 'actually happened'. History, Geography. Science. True crime as opposed to made-up stuff. A one-to-one correlation to the real world. Uncomplicated.

But later as I began to read more and more non-fiction, I began to realize that my father and I had a very binary view of the book world and that it was not so simple. Realist fiction, historical fiction, fictive autobiography all use non-fiction frameworks. And non-fiction uses fictive techniques, blending these seemingly contradictory binaries into creative non-fiction, speculative biography, autobiographical fiction, etc. Fact and fiction are a fluid continuum. At university I read Robert Scholes's introduction to *The Elements of Fiction* (1969) where he explained this continuum of forms and genres by using a metaphor I found useful – narrative is a prism of truth where writers create or fracture the 'truth' into a spectrum of colours, ranging from pure fact on the one hand (which cannot be described because as soon as it is written about it becomes subjective and fictive), and pure fantasy on the other, which equally cannot be written for as soon as it is, it becomes grounded (Scholes 1969: 1). In between these two extreme forms of fiction and non-fiction, there is a range from more factual or non-fictional forms such as journalism, history, true crime on the one hand and crossing the fiction/non-fiction line, realism to fantasy. And in all this fluid range of narrative expression, Scholes points out that we are never describing things as they are in a simplistic way, that fact and fiction are the same thing – whenever we write, we are 'making' texts, whether factual or fictional, as both words come from the same root meaning: *'fingere'* (fiction) – to make, *'facere'* (fact) – to make (Scholes 1969: 1).

Even though there is a spectrum, and fact and fiction involve the same kind of making activity, Scholes is careful to draw a thick line on his continuum between fiction and non-fiction, not because there is a significance in essence but because of reader expectation and the 'Reader/Writer contract' which we will discuss a little later. When writing memoir, we may stray onto what appears to be the fictional side of the line now and then, but there's an expectation from readers that the story we are telling is *true*. Radical memoir holds to this golden standard of 'truth' but challenges traditional expectations of how truth is or should be conveyed; like fiction, memoir makes use of the writer's craft and often blurs the idea of a hard boundary between fiction and non-fiction. As writers cross these boundaries, they may play with them in refreshing ways in order to get to the 'truth'.

Shelley

Memoir is the impressionist painting of aspects of life that emotionally shift the reader into a state of empathy and understanding. Mirror neurons ensure that we live into one another's lives if those lives are portrayed viscerally, authentically, to the point where the reader is emotionally transported into the world and point of view of the protagonist. In 'Transportation into Narrative Worlds', Green (2021) identifies how good writing allows an immersive experience that closely mirrors a lived experience. The more individual and personal a memoir is, the more authentically emotional states are portrayed, and the more universally accessible the emotional narrative becomes. My particular heartbreak, for example, may occur under vastly different circumstances from yours, but if I can, through adept wordsmithing, elicit my experience finely and deftly, you will be able to immerse yourself in my rendition of heartbreak.

To me, autobiography is the writing equivalent of realist artwork: it attempts to record in great detail every aspect of the image it reflects – it is a mirror and its job is to capture realistic details, portray accurately what happened when, and how. Memoir is a play of light and colour, a pastiche of happenings that, when you step back, creates a whole image, capturing a feeling, an intense emotional landscape, though it is made up of brushstrokes that do not aim, in and of themselves, to exactly replicate the world that they capture. Think of Monet's 'Waterlilies' as a metaphor for memoir, compared with a photograph of the same pond.

What follows are some of the different forms memoir can take. Some of these would be in the 'realist' category; others would be more 'impressionist/expressionist' – non-linear collections/impressions assembled around a theme, refracting and reflecting light. Ultimately, memoir relies on literary craft that creates an authentic emotionally transportative narrative that abides by the reader/writer contract: this happened; this is what it was like.

Forms of memoir: Between realism and impressionism/expressionism

Life writing is the general category of personal 'true life' writing that broadly encompasses all the forms of memoir writing, where the reader/writer contract demands that the writing is 'true' or 'factual': creative non-fiction, autobiography, biography, memoir, diary, travel writing, autobiographical fiction, letters, collective biography, poetry, case history, personal testimony, essay, memoirs. The form tends towards realism and representation in detail, what happened when, to whom and how.

Creative non-fiction is an even broader category of 'true life' writing that need not even be personal story – an essay, a journal article, a research paper, a tweet. The main characteristic in this form (that first appears to be a contradiction in terms) is that the content is non-fiction, the form creative. There is a myriad of creative techniques that can be used to write non-fiction, such as dialogue, setting, character, plotting and narrative arcs.

Autobiography

An autobiography is literally 'self-life-writing'. Generally, autobiography is thought to be a comprehensive, whole life story from birth to the present day. If your grandfather is writing his 'memoirs' he is writing autobiography. Philippe Lejeune was the first to help make memoir and autobiography respectable and it was he who established the 'reader/writer contract' and wrote the ground rules. He defines autobiography as 'the retrospective record in prose that a real person gives of his or her own being, emphasizing the personal life and in particular the "story of life"' (Lejeune 1982: 193).

Fictional autobiography/autobiographical fiction

Fictional autobiography uses the form and conventions and guise of autobiography to tell a fictional story. Charles Dickens often used this form, for example, in the novel fiction *David Copperfield* (1849) which begins with the chapter 'I am born'. Autobiographical fiction, on the other hand, is a combination of autobiographical and fictional writing, using the writer's real-life experience but making it into a story that looks autobiographical. *The House on Mango Street* by Sandra Cisneros (1984) is a good example of this blended genre. *Freefalling* (Davidow 1992) is an autobiographical young adult novel that loosely follows the author's experience of growing up in a multiracial household during Apartheid South Africa and the death of a childhood friend. The element that sets autobiographical fiction apart from memoir is the fact that although elements of the story are held to be from real experience, there is no reader/writer contract that is expected to be fulfilled, nor can it be easily broken.

Memoir

A memoir is a sliver of your life. It's a song with a theme. Whereas autobiography attempts to cover the whole of the writer's life, memoir tends to focus on one theme or strand of their life. It is autobiographical, it is life writing, it can be creative non-fiction, it can be a diary, poetry, letters, collective but it is a particular focus, and its timeframe is limited. You could write several memoirs about your life, and they could all be completely different in theme and subject matter. Memoir draws on techniques from all forms of life-writing, and it does not necessarily promise an 'as it happened' realist version of a segment of human experience. Memoir strives, above all, for emotional truth. Memoirs were originally the domain of famous people, and typically written by (or ghost written for) celebrities and politicians and were autobiographical, but some celebrity memoirs, for example, Michelle Obama's *Becoming* (2018) and more recently *The Light We Carry* (2022), focus on a specific theme rather than an entire life. Memoir, however, is no longer a celebrity genre has now become the domain of the ordinary person and allows us to express aspects of our lives, insights or themes that others will find interesting.

Memoirs

Memoir arose out of a form called memoirs, which were comprehensive recollections by prominent figures, for example, Alfred Von Tirpitz's *My Memoirs: Recollections of a World War I German Grand Admiral* (1923), a hefty

600 pages of history around the First World War. Memoirs nowadays have negative and ageist connotations, sometimes written by wispy-haired war veterans, often self-indulgent, nostalgic and past-glorifying, and sometimes nothing more than diary or journal entries without a directed theme or focus. The term 'memoirs' has largely gone out of common use.

Radical memoir

The radical memoir challenges and questions the assumptions readers and writers may have of the memoir genre. For example, can writers break the so-called reader/writer contract and still call the work a memoir? Can a writer move beyond the binaries of fact/fiction? These questions emerge out of other valid questions such as: do we actually remember things accurately and who gets to say what is true? What is memory? Is it a recall of data stored unchanged in some part of the brain, or is every memory an act of recreation of an experience? Who is the final arbiter of the claim that 'this really happened?' And more radically, does that matter and to whom and why? A writer writing memoir might be driven to explore one of the most fundamental questions of human experience, which is: what is the self? And do we reflect on and capture that self as we write, or do we create it as we write? Examples of radical memoir are scattered through this book, as they tend to break conventions and defy expectations of what we commonly regard memoirs as. For example, Dave Eggers's memoir *A Heartbreaking Work of Staggering Genius* (2000) questions notions of memoir and deconstructs the genre as he writes it. Lisa Taddeo's bestselling novel *Three Women* (2019) is a finely crafted literary memoir that blends aspects of autobiography, biography and investigative journalism in her ground-breaking pursuit of the breadth and scope of selves, and the meaning and cost of female desire.

We invite you to use this book as a practical workshop course. It can be used in real-time writing workshops (we suggest two-hour workshops for ten weeks) or you can work through it on your own. Make sure you do and keep all the exercises so that you can collate them at the end into a portfolio of your work that traces your journey into writing the radical memoir and that may even form the draft or part of a draft of the narrative you will eventually call your memoir.

FREEWRITE 1:

Write for two minutes without stopping. Do not worry about spelling, grammar or punctuation and when the two minutes are up, stop wherever you are. Your prompt is:

　　'I want to write memoir, because …'

1

The reader/writer contract

There are as many ways to do something new as there are humans who do them. Whether you are just about to start writing a memoir, or have already written several, the next piece of work you attempt will be unique and will happen under unique and new circumstances. The work may be informed by theory, research and practice, or you may just be 'inspired', putting words to paper and figuring out afterwards what you've done. If we look back at how great literature of all kinds was created, there are usually two well-worn pathways to the production of a final work: learning from an authority or drawing from experience. In this book, we will draw on the 'learned experts' in theory, but also speak out of our own gritty experience, share our life journeys and encourage you to throw caution to the wind, be wild and unfettered in your affair with words and the way you turn your life into art.

How to ride a bicycle/write a memoir

There are two ways of learning to ride this bicycle: (1) study the history of the moped, read as many academic articles as you can on the theory of motion, physics and mechanics, maybe a biography of the person who invented the bicycle, and watch many YouTube videos on how other people have learned to ride bicycles. Speak to experts who have written their PhDs on theories about bicycle riding, the politics of bicycle riding, who have deconstructed bicycle riding. Learn about balance, air speed, tyre pressure, reasons why people ride bicycles. Become an authority on bicycle riding. Line your bookshelf with books on *Bicycle Theory, How to Ride a Bicycle*. Give lectures at university on bicycle riding. Publish papers as an expert in your field to much acclaim. (Perhaps hope no one ever asks you if you have actually ridden a bicycle.)

Or: (2) Jump on a bicycle and try it. Fall off a few times, but always just get back on and try again until you get the hang of it. Learn as you go. You may need someone to help you who has ridden before to steady the bike as you wobble around and find your balance, and if you're a kid you may need training wheels, so you don't keep falling flat on your face. But as soon as you can, take those training wheels off and ride like the wind.

Writing radical memoir isn't too different.

The authors of this book are people who have ridden those metaphorical bikes before who can perhaps steady you as you find your own balance. We've learned to write the hard way, fallen off many times. But from experience we can say that the best way to write a memoir is to write a memoir: write, fall, fail, get up, write again.

Of course, if you want to be a professional bike rider, it can be helpful and even inspiring to know the science and theory behind it, how to ride efficiently, minimize wind resistance, maximize speed and conservation of energy. As we present theories and paradigms and perspectives on the art of writing memoir, we do so only to provide as much of that as we hope is useful and inspiring. Practice and praxis, for us, comes first.

Paul

EXERCISE: *Photographic realism*

Memoir is most often regarded as a true story about yourself, like a series of photos or a movie of your life. A memoir is a snapshot of a certain aspect of your life, just as a photo captures a moment. So …

Find a photo of yourself, either a recent one, or one from when you were a child. Choose one that has some significance for you – a photo that captures a frozen moment in time that you have kept and have contemplated. Here is an example.

Figure 1.1

(1) In 250 words, describe that photo to a person who has not seen it. That is, translate it as best you can into words. Aim at pure description at this stage. Do not interpret or explain what is happening in the photo. You can give details that are not there, e.g., names, ages, etc., but your main task is to describe what is happening in the photo. Go back to that moment if you can and show us that moment. Although the photo is only using one sense (sight), add in the others if you can (sound, smell, touch, taste). Use the present tense as if it is happening now. Take us back to that moment.

Here is my description (I am the skinny boy at the back, centre, in white shorts):

Ten young people in the pool at Stu's house are posing for a photo. It's a bright sunny day and we're all squinting in the bright sunlight. We are all lean, healthy, happy. I'm out of the pool behind the others, wearing white shorts, bare chested, sitting with Stu. The other boys are also bare chested.

The girls are bunched together in the pool, wearing full bathing suits, only their head and shoulders out of the water. Everyone is smiling except for me – well I'm baring my teeth. Maybe the camera caught me at an odd moment, but I look nervous. Behind is the concrete wall screening us from the neighbours. This must be around 1975 or 1976. Rhodesia in Southern Africa. It must be summer holidays, maybe December, or earlier as it looks dry just before the summer rain hits. We spend every day of the holidays outside, swimming, cycling, lounging around in large groups. On the left is nine-year-old Alison, then sixteen-year-old Jenny (not her real name) with her arm around her sister Jean (not her real name), the three boys who are my friends, John and John. Stu is the only one of us whose parents have a pool (we consider that a rich family) and we hang around here every afternoon to play volleyball, swim, play Marco Polo. I'm eighteen, older than the others. I'm muscular, lean, fit, and handsome, but nerdy. The sun is baking hot, the smell of chlorine strong.

(2) If you are working with others, show the passage to a partner or read it out to them, but do not show them the photo. Can they 'see' the photo and experience the moment as it happened from your description of it? Now show them the photo and get their feedback on how well you described it. Did you manage to capture that moment in words as the photo captured it in an image?

(3) Appearance and reality: now let's go deeper than the surface. What was happening underneath that appearance of the photo? What were your feelings? What emotions or mood was present? What had happened before that frozen moment in time or afterwards? What is not shown here? What secrets are hidden under this façade? Write a 250-word paragraph telling us the hidden story of the photograph. Here is mine:

I am in love with Jenny, but we have a Platonic relationship because we are all part of a Baptist Church group, and sex is not allowed. Physical attraction is of the Devil, so ours has to be a spiritual relationship, even though our teenage hormones are raging (well, mine anyway – I can't speak for the others). We pray together, go to movies in groups – no dating. Definitely no kissing or even holding hands. I look sex-deprived and repressed. I am. I masturbate every night thinking about Jenny and then pray for God's forgiveness for thinking impure thoughts. I've kissed a girl once and held hands when I was sixteen but then the Lord 'convicted' me to give her up. All girls in the church are like sisters. But I'm popular: my nickname is Smiley (or Smailliw – my surname backwards). John (blonde John on the right) is the spiritual leader who monitors our behaviour, was the one who decided that dancing was evil, so our parties now consist of playing card games. Sports is a good wholesome activity, but not on Sundays.

In a year's time I will be conscripted to fight in the civil war – you wouldn't know there was a war on, would you, by the photo, and every white male will have to join the army and fight? I have no idea what is going to hit me. I'm in a bubble, a privileged, white, teenage paradise, sheltered from the world. We live in an African country where 90 per cent of the population is Black, but the only Black people we know are the live-in servants who clean our houses and trim our lawns.

---

(4) Research: do you need to do some research about how to give us a
    better picture of that frozen moment in time? What is the wider cultural
    context – social, political, psychological, philosophical, spiritual? For
    example, what year/date/place was this? Here is mine:

Around us the war is raging, but we know little of it except through the propaganda media we get on state-controlled radio and TV and newspapers. In 1976, we are losing the war and Mugabe's forces are overrunning the country, but we think we're winning. We feel smugly right. But we're so wrong. At this point white Rhodesians have one of the highest living standards in the world, but there is a vast discrepancy between white and Black. Yet Black Rhodesians have one of the highest living standards in Africa at this point and higher than they will ever be in post-independence Zimbabwe. The people in this photo probably cannot imagine that this country will become in their lifetime one of the poorest and unhappiest countries in the world with the highest inflation in the world. At present, there is zero inflation and food is abundant for everyone.

I also searched through my old school letters and found the one Jenny wrote to me at this time. (No wonder my smile in the photograph is forced!)

Dear Smiley

I am really scared to say this as I haven't a clue what your feelings are for me, but I feel that I must be totally honest with you. I have gradually lost my feelings for you. I still regard you as very special and you mean a lot to me. I am a real loss for words, but I hope and pray that you understand. God bless my friend.

Your sister in Christ

Jenny

---

(5) Now look back at the photo from your present perspective. How do you feel about that person/event/situation now? Do you see it/yourself differently now? What is different? Write a paragraph that assesses/evaluates/judges that slice of time. Here's mine:

I was lost at the time this photo was taken and did not plan for the future. John became a wealthy oil magnate; the other John and Stu became church ministers, stayed on in Zimbabwe and Jenny went to Bible college. I was conscripted into the army and fought in the war for two years, but the other boys somehow managed to avoid the compulsory military service. John did his service in South Africa, the other John went to USA to Bible College. I was the only one who left the church and became an atheist. Back then, I had a low self-image and no self-confidence and was trapped in a conservative, sexist, racist, fundamentalist worldview that did not serve me well.

I note too that in those days we had no phones, no internet, no social media. No Western material consumer goods. Rhodesia was cut off from the world by sanctions. We spent our days outdoors playing with friends, cycling, swimming, walking, going to movies once a week, to parties (no dancing, alcohol, sex or drugs, however).

> (6) Destabilizing memory: do you think there are any inaccuracies in how you have described yourself/this event/these people? Any biases you have or had? Write a short paragraph discussing this. Here's mine:

My bias is that now from my present-day perspective, I think I missed out on life. I could have had lots of relationships, joined a rock band, experimented with different lifestyles, experienced life to the fullest. But maybe I was protected from a disastrous life of drugs, debauchery, alcohol. I don't know. If I was to go back I would certainly live it differently. And maybe I'm unjustly bitter that I had to go to war, and they all avoided it. And maybe I am being harsh on that boy who was me.

> (7) What did you learn about yourself by doing this exercise? Any insights you have discovered? Can you sum up who you are? Who you were? Have you changed? How? Why? What point could you make about yourself here? What did you focus on? Is there a theme? Write a paragraph analysing this. Here's mine:

I was naïve and propagandised, sheltered. I was arrogant in the surety of my beliefs and within six months all that would come crashing down around me. It was like being on the *Titanic* blissfully unaware that my whole ship was going to sink before I had had a chance to enjoy being on it. I had to remake myself. I am a different person now and find it hard to relate to who that younger version of me was.

> (8) FORM: now put this all together and write a conclusion. Here's what I did:

Look at the eighteen-year-old boy at the back of the photo, grimacing into the camera. He is insecure, shy, a virgin, and does not know who he is or what to do with his life, how to have relationships with women. I wish I could go back and tell him, but would I have the heart to say that he would be bullied in the army, his friends would die in front of him, he would lose the country he loves, he would live in exile all over the world, that he would get so hurt by relationships that he would put up a glass wall around his heart so that he would not ever have to feel pain or loss again? But I would also tell him his future would be an adventure, that he would live on five continents and find unexpected treasures along the way …

Congratulations! You have started writing your memoir. You jumped on that bicycle and rode it.

Autoethnography

We write memoir for a number of reasons. Perhaps all of those reasons have their root in the shortest memoir ever written: *I was here*. Beyond that, there's an intrinsic desire to share, but also, and sometimes this is subconscious, to re-create ourselves, to turn our lives into art and process events that shaped us. In this sense, memoir-writing can be a form of therapy that helps writers understand themselves.

When we make ourselves the subject of our creative 'investigation', we create a character, a self that is separate from the writing self – the character is observed living, responding to and experiencing a society and others around them.

Academics at universities often refer to certain examinations of ourselves, certain reflections and analyses of ourselves in our context, as autoethnography – the study of ourselves in society. Autoethnography is a recognized qualitative research method where a writer uses self-reflection and personal experience to understand who they are in a wider cultural context – social, political, psychological, philosophical, spiritual (Pace 2012: np). My photo memoir was autoethnographic in that it was an attempt to understand my eighteen-year-old self in a political, sexual, spiritual, social, psychological, cultural context. This is rewarding because it gives us dimension and context and deepens any memoir from mere description to a more radical understanding of 'self'.

When we think of writing memoir, we often think it is just writing down our memories. But to make it rich and authentic, we may end up doing research that falls under the theoretical banner of 'autoethnography'. This involves the use the data collecting methods such as participant observation (analysing our memories), interviews (with family members, friends to get another perspective) conversational engagement (talking to others about this incident), narrative and artefact analysis (e.g. me getting out the letters Jenny wrote to me at that time and analysing them), archival research (researching the events of that time), journaling, field notes (going back to the places I am writing about and observing details). This is an exciting part of the research into yourself.

Reader/writer contract

Rule # 1 in memoir is that the writer never breaks the reader/writer contract. That contract is: 'this is a true story'. The reader-writer contract is not written down anywhere. But it is assumed by every reader when they pick up a book that is categorized as non-fiction, or memoir or autobiography or true crime.

Simply put, readers expect that the writer did not make this stuff up, that it is 'true', factually correct, that the writer is being as accurate as possible, that the writer is not telling lies, 'telling stories, fibs, whoppers', that what the author describes 'actually happened'. Similar to a journalist's code of ethics, writers of memoir swear to tell the truth, nothing but the truth, so help them God – or, to be honest, to tell their version of the truth, with the implicit understanding that subjective truths can (and will) often be contested by others who experienced things differently.

Look at my depiction of my eighteen-year-old self. How accurate is that description? Am I biased in my retelling of it? Of course. I could have told it a different way. The second thing to bear in mind is that we shape our memoirs using literary techniques, to make the story flow. This is good memoir literary practice. I told my photo story as a narrative using techniques such as foreshadowing, setting, character description and plot.

The reader/writer contract is about telling the truth, but is this actually possible? In the previous exercises, you selected certain facts, omitted others, interpreted them. How accurate was your description? Was it 100 per cent honest and true?

Let's imagine a reader-writer contract. What would it look like?

1   The author, protagonist and narrator are the same person.

2   If the book is advertised as non-fiction, every 'fact' is verifiable.

3   The writer portrays events as accurately as possible.

4   The writer is accountable and answerable for claims made in the book.

5   Memoir writers will strive to recall memories as accurately as possible and do research to fact-check them.

6   Writers will be as honest as possible.

7   Writers can in no circumstances make up things, put in stories that are not true or exaggerate events, or embellish incidents.

There are some immediate problems with these rules. Can you change names of people to protect their identities? Can you leave out things that are not important? For example, it is a fact that you go to the toilet several times a day, but is it necessary to tell us this unless it serves the story in some way? Can you conflate events that are similar? Can you make up dialogue that approximates a conversation you had? Can you shape the 'ebb and flow' of events, create character arcs and plot tension in order to make sense of life, which is often not ordered and random and chaotic?

The answer is yes, as long as the reader knows you are doing that and understands how you shape your memoir. The reader/writer contract includes the understanding that you need to shape facts into narrative, and this means leaving things out, contracting long boring repeat episodes, even making two characters one, giving approximate dialogue – in other words, using narrative techniques that are common to writing fiction. Memoir is telling a story after all, not listing events, and if we are telling a story we need to use those story telling tools to make our memoirs work. No one wants to just read a list of events that occurred to you.

The other issue is that getting to the absolute truth is not possible, so it is better to acknowledge that subjectivity is at the heart of memoir. The memoir is not the thing itself, not the actual event. A memoir is by its very nature a 'memory', not 'what happened to me' but a subjective account of what happened.

And if subjectivity is at the heart of memoir, it is an Impressionist painting more than a photograph.

The reader/writer contract presented above is therefore an impossible ask. We push those boundaries as memoir writers every day – but if we go too far, we are on the borderlands of fiction – and it might serve the reader and writer to rather call the work autobiographical fiction – or even a novel as both authors have done with some of their memoirs.

Marcel Proust tried to give a scientific memory recall in his *A la recherche de temps perdu* (*In Search of Lost time*) (Proust 1913–27) where he attempted to capture as accurately as possible the past exactly as he remembered it. But it is a ponderously lengthy book coming in at a staggering 4,215 pages, seven volumes, 1,267,069 words (Valentine 2015: np). It is impossible to capture every detail of your memory and even if you did, who would want to read it?

Truth is always mediated and selective and therefore subjective and from a biased perspective. And this is a good thing. It makes it interesting and personal.

If another person wrote about your photo (e.g. someone else who was in the photo, like Jenny) – they would write a completely different narrative. Even if you wrote the same memoir at another time in your life, it would be different. But it would not be any less 'true.'

Philippe Lejeune

Philippe Lejeune (1938–) is the 'father' of modern autobiography and established the ground rules for writing forms of memoir and autobiography, delineated the 'reader/writer contract' or what he calls '*le pacte autobiographique*' and clarified the relationship of author, narrator, protagonist and reader for the writer of memoirs. The crucial heart of this pact is that the author, narrator and protagonist of the life writing (autobiography, memoir) are the exact same identity. 'What defines autobiography for the one who is reading is above all a contract of identity that is sealed by the proper name. And this is true also for the one who is writing the text' (Lejeune 1989: 19). This is crucial. If the author says in their memoir, *yes, this happened to me, I am that person*, we hold them to that contract.

But even so, Lejeune admits that it is an illusion that we can tell the truth about ourselves: 'telling the truth about the self, constituting the self as complete subject – it is a fantasy', but 'in spite of the fact that autobiography is impossible, this in no way prevents it from existing' (131–2). What he argues is that 'autobiography identity grounds resemblance' (24), meaning that we can only approximate our identity in writing.

Lejeune also defines autobiography (and this equally applies to memoir) as 'a discourse on the self' in which 'the question, "who am I?" is answered by a narrative that tells "how I became who I am"' (124). Memoir and autobiography tell the story of how I became myself, this person I call 'I'. It also allows the writer agency over a life lived, and how it is seen; it allows us to 'shape' who we are: 'We are never really the cause of our life, but we can have the illusion of becoming its author by writing it' (192).

Who am I?

Paul

If you want to know who someone is, these days you Google them, look them up on social media and find out what they have done, look at photos of them, their history, their friends. We now create inadvertent digital autobiographies of ourselves online. We also sometimes create conscious autobiographies of ourselves online, on dating sites, in blogs, on platforms like LinkedIn, Wikipedia and on our personal websites. But is this really you, or me? Each 'presence' is a character, created, constructed, in order to leave a certain impression.

Shelley

We all have constructed selves. Some of them live out there on social media platforms. There might be several different platforms projecting entirely different and even conflicting selves out into the ether. Imagine, for example, a young teacher at a private school whose Facebook and Instagram account portray her as a conservative, home-focused graduate who loves her dog and walks on the beach for entertainment. But she also has a TikTok account under a different name in which she is a wild party animal who pushes the boundaries and lives life on the edge. Which one of these is the true person? Are both of them true? Are both of them constructs? What happens when people discover that the two versions of this person are the same individual – does that mean the person is a liar?

We are inherently story-makers, and social media platforms give us the opportunities to create numerous versions of ourselves. The people that others 'follow' on social media are always constructs. Details are added, omitted, changed, to suit an observer, reader or community, and yet we all too often believe in their 'truth' for better or worse. This is true to a degree of every human interaction. The self I present at a conference to colleagues is perhaps different to the self I am when running on the beach and stopping to chat to a friend. The 'truth' of the 'self' is a mysterious, multifaceted and I believe, continuously evolving thing.

EXERCISE: *The Truth is …*

Do an internet search on yourself and see what your digital 'self' looks like today. There may be almost no information, or there may be lots. Write a 150-word paragraph about yourself based on that information. Now add another paragraph beginning, 'the truth is …' with details about yourself that may contradict some of what you've found online.

Speed dating

For those who have tried, the hardest exercise in honest self-definition is to write a dating profile of yourself for a dating site. Usually the app requires photos of you, your interests, occupation, physical description, temperament, and may include some psychological survey. It is easy, and often expedient, prudent, to create a false image of yourself, put yourself in your best light, photoshop your photo, use filters and touch up your profile. Creating a profile reveals how fictional the process of autobiography is – we need to create a self, a positive, likeable image of who we are, portray an avatar of ourselves. How often have dates turned out badly when the 'real' person does not match the construction of the self on the dating site!

EXERCISE: *Speed dating*

Write a 250-word profile of yourself as you would want it to appear on a dating site and insert a photo of yourself to match. Create this profile where you are seen in the best, most attractive possible light. Use dating site guidelines if it helps.

Now write another 250-word profile, but this time be as searingly honest as you can, describing all your faults; insert a photo that is a reflection of that self.

What is the effect of these two versions of you side-by-side? Could this be a useful literary device in your memoir?

Conclusion

Memoir and autobiography, if it is to obey the reader/writer contract, needs to be 'true'. The problem, of course, is that your truth is subjective. Only you have your unique experience of the world. This gives rise to interesting dilemmas. Perhaps the act of writing a memoir becomes a journey in the confronting of truth, perceptions of yourself, of the past; it is possible that the act of writing yourself into your memoir may end up evolving your understanding of who you are, illuminating aspects of yourself that lay in shadow. And this may be valuable, an unexpected discovery on the journey you take in writing your story into the world.

2

Memoir as cartography: Mapping your life

Shelley

A Lakota Elder once said: 'Everything. Everything is story' (Baumeister, RF and LS Newman 1994: 676). We tell stories from the minute we can talk. We wake up and tell a partner a dream. We meet for coffee with friends and tell them stories of things that have happened. We are narrative creatures, primed to make sense of our world – to connect the dots – to build the plot. We all have stories about ourselves.

Dr Lewis Mehl-Madrona is a narrative psychiatrist whose practice and research show that sometimes changing the interior narrative of his patients' lives actually changes their lives and the way they live them. He suggests that internal narratives are underpinned by overarching themes, such as *bad things always happen to me* or *I'm always lucky* or *I get away with things*. These primary narratives are stories that become entrenched neurological patterns that can in fact, be shifted over time (Mehl-Madrona 2015).

We believe that these primary narratives have a deep influence on the tone and manner in which we construct our memoirs. For example, if you are writing about something that's recently happened, and you are generally a person who feels like life has treated you unfairly, it's hard to create art without running the risk of your work ending up as a 'poor me' 'misery memoir'.

Whatever understory we hold about ourselves, being aware of it can help us as writers to create narratives that don't sink – that pick up on themes, allowing readers to identify with the characters, the journey, as they would with a good, gripping novel.

We get to choose how we view and construct our lives. There's no objective, all-encompassing 'this is the way things are', that we can draw on because we can never get outside ourselves, outside of the solar system to look back at the whole picture. We can, however, be authentic about our perceptions of the way things are – the truth of how things are, from our point of view and try to step outside our habit narrative patterns that make us see ourselves a certain way. Meaning in terms of our own lives, is mapped and made by the meaning-maker: me, or you.

Treasure map of the self

Paul

I was always a fan of graphs and maps and diagrams. As a child I was always drawing charts. I charted the rise and fall of my favourite songs on the hit parade, I listed my friends in similar fashion, and most significantly, I mapped my own emotional terrain and charted out my life in terms of what I called my 'happiness index'. On the 'x' axis were the years since I was born, and the 'y' axis was the amount of happiness measured in percentages. For example, as a child my happiness line was up towards the 100 per cent mark, but then when puberty hit, it dropped below zero into negative territory. When I first fell in love, it soared, then when this person (inadvertently) broke my heart, it plummeted again. My teenage years were full of crises and high points, dipping when I began high school and was immersed into a bullying culture, soaring when I met a Christian group, spiking higher when I fell in love, plunging when she rejected me, jumping again at my first kiss …

I didn't realize it then, but I was writing my emotional memoir, not in words, but with a scientific measuring tool. What was useful was that I could remember and pinpoint the turning points in my life, the crises, the high and lows, the patterns and the journey I was embarking on. A soul adventure, perhaps. I could look back and see where I was happiest, and why, where the

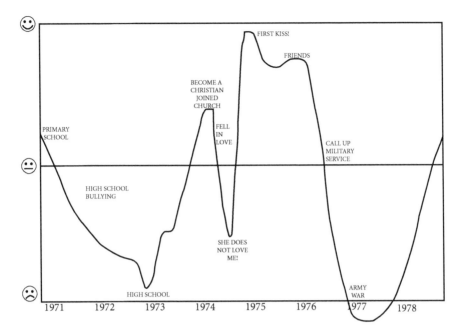

Figure 2.1 *Happiness index chart.*

life crises were and how I dealt with them. I could see the shape of my life as it was unfolding before me, see how I was turning out. *First Kiss. Death of a friend. Exam results. University. Friendship. Love. First real job. Achievements. First book published.* It was all subjective of course, more about my feelings about how things were rather than external events. During the civil war in Rhodesia, for example, I was happy in spite of the political turmoil because I had found a community where I felt loved (and maybe was living in denial!)

EXERCISE: *Happiness index graph*

Make a graph of your emotional life with an x and y axis. x is time (age three to now); y is happiness. Place 4 or 5 or more pivotal events on your timeline. Now use each of these as a heading and write rough notes about each of these major events. When you are done, make some reflective notes on whether you have any revelations or insights into the pattern of your life. Is there a story there?

I always wanted to write my autobiography and did not realize that I had already plotted it in my life graph – here was my planned map of the territory I could write about. The next step was easy – to select crucial turning points and tell my story in words. Here's one:

First Kiss

I was 16. She was 14. It happened so unexpectedly. I was charting at the bottom of the graph that summer holiday, below zero, because I had fallen in love with Frances, a girl who had rejected me. She 'just wanted to be friends' and so was still hanging around our group, which of course made it worse. Our group (all ten of us) went to the movies, and Frances sat on my left. But on my right was a bright girl called Heather, new to the group, who chatted to me and in the course of the movie, took hold of my hand and caressed it. I was so surprised that I did not know what to do and went along with it. We walked home hand in hand to the shocked silence of the others (and myself). The girl (Frances) who had broken my heart stared at us all the way home. We all went back to my parents' house and somehow I ended up in our living room where I sat alone with Heather on the couch, and the others went into the kitchen to make coffee. Again, before I knew it, she was kissing me. My first kiss. I had never experienced anything like it. Her lips. The tip of her tongue. Her sweet breath. The tickle of her brown hair on my face. Her eyes and freckles close up. My heart fluttered. I was in complete ecstasy, felt as if I had taken an overdose of some hallucinogenic drug, my senses spilled over, I felt weak, I felt like all lovers who had ever lived, connected to all the poets throughout the centuries who had fallen in love, and felt 'this is it', this is the centre of the universe, the meaning of life.

But at that moment, as I opened my eyes to see her sweet face, over her shoulder I saw in horror that the others were staring at us, laughing, making imitation smooching noises. And Frances – the girl who had rejected me only a day before – was wide eyed, shocked, disturbed, broken hearted even. I was paralysed, lips still attached. Heather did not know, continued to kiss me. 'They're … watching us,' I whispered.

'Forget about them,' she said. 'They're just jealous.'

After that, we became an inseparable item for months, and the girl who had rejected me, who had shunned me, suddenly became over friendly, my best friend, wanting to see me, calling me on the phone every evening 'just to chat', writing me notes and letters. I was puzzled. I had no idea. And for years after, even after I broke up with Heather, Frances followed me around, my 'best friend', flirting, even, and making what I thought were maybe hints that we should 'go out'. But I was unforgiving. She had broken my heart. I would never let her in again.

That first kiss was when my graph reached its first peak since I had been at high school and stayed at that peak for the remaining school years.

EXERCISE: *First Kiss*

Using the First Kiss Example, choose a significant event from your graph (crisis point, peak, trough) and write a scene (300 words) that illustrates the underlying theme of that event.

Bias

I talked about a 'scientific method' of chronicling my life using charts and graphs, but of course this will be inevitably biased because it will be viewed from the present. And we tend to look back with sentimental nostalgia or with judgemental harshness at our past selves. It cannot be avoided, but we can be aware of this and acknowledge our biases. We could even write two versions of the same event from different perspectives and at different times. And looking back you might see things that you did not see then. For example, my first kiss was at sixteen but I did not kiss anyone else until seven years later. I soon broke up with Heather preferring to be polyamorous rather than one half of a monogamous couple; I felt she was restricting my freedom to be with others. Not that I slept around. I remained a virgin, keeping everyone at arm's length until I was twenty-three. I look back now at that first kiss with nostalgia, and judgement about my cruel break-up with her. But by writing about that moment in time, I begin to understand something about myself and how it formed me. I was passive when it came to relationships, let things happen to me. I was also (what would be called today) a relationship anarchist.

Reflecting on an event you have written about is also good practice. It helps shape and form the theme of your memoir and give it direction.

EXERCISE: *The rear-view mirror*

Reflecting on that significant event, write a retrospective from the present in a short paragraph (200 words): what does this event reveal about you? Is there a theme? How has that theme played out in your life following that event? What will unfold in the future of the person you were?

Freytag's pyramid

We always look for patterns to make sense of our lives. We tell the story of our life, usually with a beginning, middle, end, with crisis, conflict and hopefully, resolution. Think about when you tell your friends some incident that happened to you – it forms itself into a narrative with a beginning, middle, end, a punchline, a surprise maybe, a climax, a point. All stories have a pattern, and it is a surprisingly regular one. Gustav Freytag (1816–95), a German novelist, identified this pattern diagrammatically, in what is now known and Freytag's pyramid. A story begins with an introduction, a setting of the scene, and the drive of the story. The thrust of the story is the 'inciting incident' that begins the 'complication' where some force sets the protagonist into motion. The 'rising action' of the story builds to a 'climax' at the apex of the pyramid where things fall apart or reach a head, and all action rises to this moment, and then begins falling away from into a 'falling action' before the final 'catastrophe' or 'unravelling' or 'denouement' or the story's final outcome.

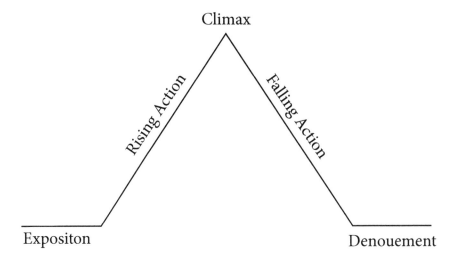

Figure 2.2 *Freytag's pyramid.*

Most stories roughly follow this pattern or rise and fall, and most Hollywood movies do too. It is a formula that works and helps us make sense of the world in terms of a satisfying pattern of rise and fall. For example, look at any story or novel and plot the narrative on a graph and it will on average form itself into a pyramid shape. Even the way we tell anecdotes or yarns follows this pattern.

EXERCISE: *My life as a pyramid*

Plot your proposed memoir on this pyramid chart. What's the inciting event? What is the climax? What's the resolution? See the example below and use the headings if they are useful.

Paul

Here's one of my narratives. People often ask me how I became a university lecturer/professor, and I tell them this story, which naturally fell into the neat pattern of beginning, middle, end, premise or tagline, just as if it were a fictional story.

Tagline/hook

I became a university lecturer/professor by pure chance.

Exposition

I always wanted to teach at university. I completed a Bachelor degree then Honours then a Master's degree. I applied for university jobs, but never got one. I suspected I was just not good enough, not cut out to be an academic. I applied for a teaching position at a local university, but it was my friend Craig who got the position. I fell into a depression, gave up my ambition.

Inciting incident

To cure my depression and feeling of inadequacy, I headed off to a dance club on Saturday night, and lo and behold there was Craig, dancing away, drinking beer. I felt a pang of envy – he had always been the better intellectual and so of course he had got the job I coveted. If only I could just be given a chance to prove myself, I thought. But I never got the chance.

Rising action

I greeted him and he called me over to drink beer with him. I met his friends and we danced. 'Congrats on the job,' I said. Then he hit me with the bombshell. 'I can't take it,' he said, 'I've been conscripted and if I don't go, I'll be arrested and put in jail.'

'So what about the job?'
'They think I'm starting on Monday. I haven't told them yet.'

Climax

He grabbed my shoulder. 'Why don't you call Tony Voss, Head of English, and tell him you can take my place.'

'I can't do that.'
'Of course you can. Here's his number.'

I wished Craig luck in the army, and the next day, I called Professor Voss, nervous as hell, told him that I was available. 'Thank God,' he said. 'I didn't know what to do. We have two hundred restless students expecting classes on Douglas Livingstone's poetry. Can you start Monday morning? And are you familiar with Livingstone's work?'

'Sure,' I said. And spent the day frantically reading Douglas Livingstone's poetry for the first time.

Falling action

I was nervous, but gave the lecture, took the tutorials and started the job. It went well. I was a temporary lecturer, until they could re-advertise the position. I moved to Mtunzini and settled into the job.

Resolution or denouement

That was the break I needed. I started publishing papers and kept the job for two years. They didn't advertise the job straight away, as it turned out, and it began my career as a university lecturer. I never looked back. And all because of a chance meeting at a night club, and conscription.

I am not sure if life is really always like that, or we impose a narrative structure on our life journey to make sense of it. But for me there were some defining Freytag pyramid moments where problems were resolved, crises occurred and worked out. I have shared two happy ending stories, but of course they could be tragedies that end in disaster too. I have written those into stories too, for example, one short story about how we found a perfect dream house to live in, but how it was cheated out of us, and we lost it (published as '31 Murdering Creek Road' in *Tincture Journal*, 2015). As with charting your life on a graph, imposing or finding neat narrative structures in your past life is necessarily biased. We tell stories about ourselves to make sense of the world not necessarily because that is the way they actually happened, but as a meaning-making activity.

Epiphany

The heart of the structure of a narrative, the climax, the denouement, is the insight or change in the protagonist's life, some resolution, or solution to a problem. Both the above stories could be reframed as problem/solution stories. The psychologist Abraham Maslow calls the thrust on our life journey a quest for self-actualization, becoming your full self. Life is a series of challenges and problems and struggles we are trying to resolve in order to better ourselves, reach self-fulfilment, self-realization and achieve self-actualization. Whether we get there or not is another story, but there may be minor triumphs, peaks and troughs, losses and failures and successes, all of which we can use to understand who we are and try to learn from those mistakes or misfortunes. And write about them. This is what makes good memoir, not a mere recounting of events, or recording of memory, but a radical look at the underlying structures of our lives, the profound moments of insight we have about ourselves and the shape of our destiny on our journey to self-actualization.

Maslow describes the peak of self-actualization or self-realization as follows:

Feelings of limitless horizons opening up to the vision, the feeling of being simultaneously more powerful and also more helpless than one ever was before, the feeling of ecstasy and wonder and awe, the loss of placement in time and space with, finally, the conviction that something extremely important and valuable had happened, so that the subject was to some extent transformed and strengthened even in his daily life by such experiences.

(Carrano 2009: 270)

Each moment of insight or peak experience is another name for what James Joyce calls an 'epiphany' or 'aha' moment of self-realization. The Joycean epiphany has been defined as 'a sudden spiritual manifestation, whether from some object, scene, event, or memorable phase of the mind – the manifestation being out of proportion to the significance or strictly logical relevance of whatever produces it' (Beja 1971:18). When the story reaches its apex, the paradigm shifts. Joyce gives a number of examples in his works, most notably in his story 'Araby' (1914) which is autobiographical in form (if not content), about a boy who falls in love and romanticizes the situation to such an extent that he sees himself on a quest, only to be disillusioned by the ordinariness of the situation at the end, and his epiphany is one of disappointment when he realizes his place in the universe, who he is: 'Gazing up into the darkness, I saw myself as a creature driven and derided by vanity; and my eyes burned with anguish and anger' (Joyce 1914).

Most stories have a moment of epiphany. Another classic example is the John Updike story 'A&P' (1961) where the protagonist, much like the boy in 'Araby' has a deluded sense of his own hero status in trying to impress some girls who have walked into the store and once his delusions crashed, he 'felt how hard the world was going to be to [him] hereafter' (Updike 1961).

Similarly, Kate Chopin's 'Story of an Hour' (1894) which follows Freytag's pyramid structure exactly, by the way, reveals Mrs Mallard's epiphany when she realizes that her husband's death means that she is 'free, free, free' (Chopin 1894).

There would be no one to live for during those coming years; she would live for herself. There would be no powerful will bending hers in that blind persistence with which men and women believe they have a right to impose a private will upon a fellow-creature. … "Free! Body and soul free!" she kept whispering.

(Chopin 1894)

An 'epiphany' is a section of a Catholic mass, and originally refers to the revelation of the resurrected Jesus to the Gentiles. But James Joyce used it in the sense of a spiritual revelation. The best example in Joyce's work of an epiphany is the crisis apex of the pyramid in *Portrait of the Artist as a Young Man* (2000) when Stephan Daedalus who is about to become a celibate priest, sees a semi-naked woman walking on the beach and has a revelation that he will become a 'priest of the imagination', a writer!

> He turned away from her suddenly and set off across the strand. His cheeks were aflame; his body was aglow; his limbs were trembling. On and on and on and on he strode, far out over the sands, singing wildly to the sea, crying to greet the advent of the life that had cried to him.

> Her image had passed into his soul for ever and no word had broken the holy silence of his ecstasy. Her eyes had called him and his soul had leaped at the call. To live, to err, to fall, to triumph, to recreate life out of life! A wild angel had appeared to him, the angel of mortal youth and beauty, an envoy from the fair courts of life, to throw open before him in an instant of ecstasy the gates of all the ways of error and glory. On and on and on and on!
>
> (Joyce 2000: 171–2)

Paul

My English teacher at High School read us this passage and then asked us to write our own epiphanies, or spiritual revelations. Mine at the time was that I had, like Joyce, realized that my vocation was to be an artist, a 'priest of the imagination'. I rejected what I regarded as the 'boring' school Science subjects and took to English. There was no Art, Music, Film, Creative Writing subjects at our school, but I realized then that I wanted to be a writer, musician, film maker, artist, a 'priest of the imagination'.

Epiphanies can be major life-changing events, but they can also be small, and they can also happen every day. That's perhaps the difference between fiction and memoir. Writing memoir seems to involve illuminating and meditating on the undulating and potentially forgettable fabric of everyday life, and to find within it that which is sublime, a life-changing but quiet epiphany – something that no one else would notice because it is a part of a unique life.

Shelley

It's interesting to look at what other writers do with their memoirs and what constitutes an 'epiphany.' For example, I'm inspired by Hisham Mater's memoir *The Return* (2016), which is about the protagonist's quest to find out what happened to his father. The writing is as beautiful as any literary fiction – and the plot does not conclude in any neat resolution where all ends are tied up, because the work is a segment of a complex life, and the energy that propels the reader forward is the emotional trajectory of the protagonist. I strive for that in my own work, and it is important to find books and stories that ask you to be a better, truer, more dedicated worker of words. Mater's relentless quest to discover the truth about his father's disappearance results in the kind of epiphany that is so personal it becomes universal. Whether the protagonist finds the truth about his father is not the important aspect of the story. How he moves his readers to empathy and exhilaration is an epiphany moment – one in which I believe he succeeds in harnessing all the beauty of words put together just right, to convey the essence of what it means to be human:

> Grief is not a whodunnit story, or a puzzle to solve, but an active and vibrant enterprise. It is hard, honest work. It can break your back. It is part of one's initiation into death and – I don't know why, I have no way of justifying it – it is a hopeful part at that. What is extraordinary is that, given everything that has happened, the natural alignment of the heart remains towards the light.
>
> (Mater 2016: 167)

Some memoirs read like high-speed thrillers or emotional dramas with perfect plots, radical epiphanies and happy endings (e.g. *Mao's Last Dancer* by Li Cunxin), but for the most part, a memoir is an impressionist rendition of a segment of life or experience, that does not rely on a gripping external plot to drive the story, but rather on the protagonist's (your) movement towards growth and illumination, and your ability to reflect that in a compelling way.

EXERCISE: *Epiphany*

Using the chart to pinpoint an epiphany or moment of self-realization, write a 300–500-word piece story that reflects that moment. Use Matar's or Joyce's piece as inspiration.

Maslow's hierarchy of needs

If we are really honest, humans are driven by the desire to exist, to survive. We mentioned self-actualization earlier. A memoir could be any of these things: a struggle to survive, stay alive (physical journey), reach enlightenment (spiritual journey), self-understanding (psychological journey), self-control, success (material journey), life balance, freedom (political journey).

Abraham Maslow (1943) sets out a life journey path is terms of human 'needs' and this may be useful to you as you consider what is the main driver for your memoir – because perhaps there is only ever one plot in the world for every single story: *somebody wants something.*

Here are Maslow's hierarchy of needs in order of importance for survival – and for the memoir writer contemplating what kind of a book they are planning to write.

1   Physiological needs – the most important because we cannot function without air, food, drink, shelter, clothing, warmth, sex, sleep in order to survive.

2   Safety needs – We need order, predictability, control, emotional and financial security in order to flourish.

3   Love and belongingness needs – we need relationships and connectedness to others.

4   Esteem needs – we need self-esteem, self-worth, a sense of accomplishment and reputation.

5   Self-actualization needs – we need to realize our full potential, use our talents, be the best that we can be.

Your life journey then is not just a need to be self-actualized or psychologically whole, but possibly a more basic struggle for survival. Maybe yours is a struggle against poverty, ill health, disability. Maybe you and your family have become physically displaced by war, economics, religious persecution. These are all hero's journeys. The power lies in how you show the need, rather than tell it.

EXERCISE: *Every character wants something*

Write a 200-word paragraph about an intrinsic need – describe an event or incident that reflects you trying to find someone, to be loved, heard, fed, seen, to succeed, be yourself.

Conclusion

This chapter asks you to stand back and look for patterns in your life, and to use those patterns to structure your memoir. It is useful to use graphs and pyramid structures to shape your experiences, look for highs and lows, losses and victories, failures and successes, epiphanies and confusions. It's also useful to look towards other writers whose words lift us, ask us to work towards the truth, to transform as we tell our stories. The raw material of our lives has to be chiselled or shaped or moulded to become a coherent and inviting narrative.

3

The hero's journey – and beyond

Every story, to some degree or another, is a hero's journey. The hero in the memoir is you, though there may be other heroes in your life journey as well, because we live our lives not in isolation, but tangled with others, with their stories. Our needs and their needs collide. Your need to tell your story may collide with the needs of others in your life to have their stories kept silent, or to tell their part in their words, and this is where the territory of memoir becomes tricky, hazardous even. But that does not mean that the hero-memoir-writer should be faint of heart, or just give up, or change as much as possible and call the book a novel!

Freytag may have set out his plot structure for narratives in 1863, but Joseph Campbell (1904–87) had a much more ambitious quest, and that was to find the archetypal pattern of *all* stories, what he called the monomyth. *The Hero with a Thousand Faces* chronicles this discovery that all stories and mythical narratives follow the same formula, that is, the journey of the archetypal hero shared by world mythologies. This pattern, it seems, is deeply engrained in the human psyche in all cultures and times, and is closely allied to Jung's archetypes, Maslow's notion of self-actualization, Freytag's pyramid structure and hopefully the graph of your life journey. Taking the word from James Joyce (whose novel *Ulysses* 1922, is a hero's journey), Joseph Campbell called this archetypal story the 'monomyth' Campbell believed that we are constantly making meaning of our lives by transcending the mundane and making the world 'transparent to transcendence' (Campbell 2004: 1) by using metaphors and myths to shape our understanding of this yearning for meaning. The most common story of this yearning for transcendence comes in the form of 'the hero's journey', a story about a person who struggles and suffers to transcend their ordinary life and goes on a quest to find some 'eternal source', returning with an elixir, grail or gift which has the power to heal, free, enlighten people. Or in other words, they set out to solve a problem, resolve a crisis, heal a wound and return with the solution, a denouement, medicine.

Campbell called the various versions of the story 'masks', but the basis story remains the same:

1. *Ordinary World* – what Freytag calls the beginning. Life as normal.

2. *Call to Adventure* – the 'hero'/protagonist is propelled into an adventure or journey by some crisis which disrupts their normal life.

3. *Refusal of The Call* – the reluctant hero thinks the challenge is too daunting.

4. *Meeting the Mentor* – the hero receives guidance from some mentor who gives them the tools or powers to be able to make the journey.

5. *Crossing the Threshold* – the Hero begins their quest and leaves the familiar world to follow the quest into unfamiliar territory.

6. *Tests, Allies, Enemies* – the hero now faces a series of challenges (the rising action) that tests them and they must overcome each one to continue the journey. Their powers and resolve are tested.

7. *Approach to the Inmost Cave* – the hero now faces the ultimate danger, crisis or test and must prepare for the final ordeal.

8. *Ordeal* – the hero now faces the ultimate test, danger, enemy and needs to use all their resources, powers, gifts, strength and integrity to face the crisis, to overcome the problem, fight the enemy. Often this is in the form of a death and rebirth, resurrection.

9. *Reward (Seizing the Sword)* – the hero wins, defeats the evil, the enemy and emerges victorious with the prize, the elixir, the solution, the healing.

10. *The Road Back* – the hero now needs to retrace their steps back home and return with the grail/elixir to recognition, acclaim, vindication, absolution, exoneration.

11. *Return with The Elixir* – the return back to the Ordinary World, transformed, self-realized, self-actualized.

(Campbell 1949)

You may recognize this structure as the classic Hollywood movie plot, and many screenwriters have used this formula to write successful storylines (e.g. George Lucas consciously plotted *Star Wars* this way).

We can apply this structure to our own life story too, see ourselves as the hero of our lives. Why watching movies and reading stories of the hero's journey is cathartic is that it echoes the need in us to be that hero, to solve problems in our lives, to take the journey to self-actualization. Can you see this pattern anywhere in your life's journey? Are you on this journey now? Have you done this journey in any aspect of your life before that you can recognize?

EXERCISE: *You are the hero of your story*

Jot down the answers to these questions considering the memoir you're writing or wish to write:

- What is the crisis/event that precipitates the telling of this story?
- What elements make the 'adventure' daunting?
- What elements represent 'the enemy' or the forces against which you must push?
- What inner qualities/strengths/capacities do you have as the hero on this quest?
- How will you know when you reach the end of this journey?

Once you identify these elements, keep them as notes. They will find their way into your story.

Tragedy and comedy

Beyond the hero's journey, there are deeper themes in our lives – for example, what if there is no happy ending, or indeed no ending at all (since a memoir is never the whole of a person's life and does not end at the end of that life)? Perhaps there is no victory, no obvious tying up of all loose ends.

In fact, this is most likely the case. The goal that the memoir writer works towards is something that is more subtle – it looks more like personal illumination, insight or clarity. It may be nothing more than a moment of confluence, a place to rest, to let the narrative lie. Memoirs are as much about the failures and defeats of life as the successes. Sometimes the only reward is wisdom, a new perspective, the gifts of experience, of living long enough to have seen and done things, and to have hindsight. Writing about failure will make any journey relatable. Failure is the reality of everyday life in small and big ways, and memoirs offer us as writers the opportunity to delve into the complexity of our own story and to highlight themes and archetypes in our stories that connect us to others. We don't have to idealize and superimpose myths or fairy tales on real life – their archetypes, according to Jung, live there anyway. The search for the lost person inspires many memoirs. In *The Return*, Hisham Matar looks for a lost father and the journey is not about whether he finds him or not. It is an exploration of loss and love and the meaning and ongoingness of death. In *Boy, Lost*, (2013) an Australian memoir, Kristina Olsen wonders what happened to the brother she never met and the story is not about whether she finds him or not. These aching stories draw on the same elements as the Ancient Greeks drew on when they divided the human experience into Tragedy and Comedy. In comedy, irony plays a large part, and in the end, everyone lives happily ever after, while in tragedy, people are confronted by the magnitude of their own inadequacies or flaws and face circumstances outside their own control that cannot be overcome. Modern memoirs make use of both.

Paul

My short memoir 'There Is No Hereafter' (Williams 2013), for example, describing my father's funeral, is about tragedy and failure – my father's dying wish was not to have a Catholic funeral – he had become an atheist, but because of pressure by the family, both he and I caved in and he was given the full Catholic funeral rites. I felt I had failed him and wrote about the tragedy of a broken promise in a short story that described that feeling of betrayal. It was healing to write and cathartic to explore because I could go into the wound and acknowledge my failings, and the story was an attempt to understand what had happened, and to give him propitiation. The story followed Freytag's pyramid structure and reflected the failed hero's quest. Although the story did not end happily and the 'hero' did not get victory, he came away with a sense of self-realization, an epiphany about himself and how life goes.

Shelley

My memoir *Whisperings in the Blood* (Davidow 2016) – because it is a biographical family story as well as my own memoir, ends (plot spoiler) at a point where most of the heroes of the story have died – and most of them, without apparently achieving their dreams – but I question whether achieving one's dreams is what we think it is. I know that my predecessors lived. They loved. And their dreams are being played out and held in the hands of those who came after. The memoir spans a 100-year-long journey and people live and die as they make their journeys around the world in search of home. The book attempts to honour those who went before, and to say: they were here, they mattered.

The Ancient Greeks knew that life was made up of tragedy and comedy. When I was an English teacher, I used to ask my Year 10 students whether they thought life was mostly comic or tragic. One student said: life is tragic, because we all die in the end. Another said: if you look at it from a universal way-out point of view, life is at least funny/ironic, because people live as if they won't die, premising most of what they do on this weird fiction (that we live forever).

EXERCISE: *We rise and fall*

Write a 300–500-word piece about a tragic incident from your life. Give it three stages: the beginning, in which you establish your character either through dialogue or a scene – the middle, in which you are faced with the crisis and the end, in which you resolve or consolidate that happened. The piece may be about a time when you failed or were defeated by some inner or outer challenge. Use the rise and fall structure of Freytag's pyramid (in fact this structure is highly suited to tragedy).

Shelley

Here is an example from my co-written memoir *Runaways* (2022). In this segment, the metaphor of the collapsing building reflects the struggle and crumbling of connection in a young marriage.

> One night, P and I awoke with the sound of a loud explosion.
>
> We ran out, bleary-eyed onto the balcony.
>
> In the strange night, illuminated by the orange streetlights along Al-Rayyan Road, the new building between us and the Corniche looked to be awkwardly off-centre.
>
> Another ear-drum-shattering sound.
>
> The smell of concrete.
>
> I inhaled dust. As if in slow motion, the building collapsed in on itself. A crane, caught in the fall, tipped over. A plume of orange spiralled into the night.
>
> My heart raced. 'That building,' I said. 'That whole building! It just fell down. The workers …'
>
> 'Let's go inside,' P said.
>
> 'No, I want to see it,' I said. I knew I was looking at someone's death that night. The clouds grew bigger. More slabs of concrete collapsed.
>
> 'Come on,' he said, and drew me back inside.
>
> We sat in the lounge in the hours between midnight and sunrise. 'People were in there working,' I said. P made me camomile tea.
>
> 'I know,' he said.
>
> 'I want to leave,' I said.
>
> 'I know,' he said.
>
> 'You're becoming like them,' I said.
>
> 'Like who?'
>
> 'Like all the other men here. The ones who think it's okay that their wives stay at home in these boxes.'
>
> (Davidow & Khalil 2022: 161)

I didn't set out in any way to find a metaphor – this is not contrived – it just so happened that the collapse of the building coincided with the continental drift happening in the relationship – and because we humans are meaning-makers and story-makers, writing the narrative enabled me to see that there was a connection between the inner and outer collapse of a structure previously considered 'solid'. As you write, consider that deep metaphors may emerge. Let them.

Core wounds

In many hero stories, the hero or main protagonist has a core wound, something they have to struggle to heal during their hero's journey or deal with in some way. Some rite of passage is needed to come to terms with it, heal it. But it is not only fictional heroes who have such wounds – everyone has a core wound – or more than one! Such core wounds are typically inflicted in childhood and young adulthood when we are most vulnerable, still developing, when events and our responses most easily get written into neural circuitry. Betrayal, abandonment, rejection, humiliation and injustice, a sense of not being enough, of being unlovable, inadequate, ugly, stupid … the list goes on and profoundly impacts our young selves. These wounds shape us personally and so, often, as writers we are propelled to look to these wounds, to deal with them, mask them or confront them. In fact, it may be the case that the radical memoir allows the writer to confront a 'core wound' head on and attempt to turn it into art, and in so doing, transform it.

Shelley

My first memoir, *The Eye of the Moon* (Davidow 2008), is an immigrant memoir written in small, non-chronological segments that reads perhaps more like a long prose poem than that which might traditionally be called memoir. It took me ten years and 120 rejections to find a publisher. Back then, memoir wasn't really a 'thing' and this didn't fit any category. Also, at 27,000 words, it was too short to be anything recognizable to most publishers – and all but one said they would not know how to market this. I persisted and the book was eventually accepted by a small press in Oregon in 2007. I tried at some publishers' requests to expand the narrative, to turn it into a novel, and all of this failed. It was complete as it was. Radical. Small. Without a forerunner as far as the publishers could see. I wonder if now it would be seen differently.

I want to share the point in the poetic narrative that heralds the heartbreak, the 'core wound' that is to follow. You can see it is not explicit, and deliberately so. This is my verbal attempt at impressionist art:

The African Literature Guy walks along low brick walls and balances across fallen trees. We go rock-climbing and explore caves. We allow the Nyangombe river to carry us on a rushing muddy journey into a deep rock pool where we swim against the current to get to the side. We hide from torrential rain beneath the narrow eaves of a curio shop, watching as the road turns into a river of iron oxide-red mud. I feel young. I realize for the first time in my life that I am young. For the first time I let myself remember the wrinkles, smell the smell of The Journalist's forty something years against my twenty, recall how my body contracts and goes small.

The African Literature Guy plays me his music. We climb a huge tree and go to the Balancing Rocks. We whisper across the granite and listen to each other's voices carried over a huge distance. We walk along African dirt roads in the heat of the day as lonely pick-up trucks speed by, and become two characters in the same story. His arm brushes mine once and I am dizzy. He grows larger, and I make myself small lest I frighten him away.

It was the act of making myself small that was the hardest to undo.

(Davidow 2008: 12)

In *Whisperings in the Blood*, a pivotal moment of heartbreak becomes one of the core wounds I address. By the end of the passage, I have used the third person (the besotted Jewish Girl) to embody the emotional excision I was attempting at the time. Here is that extract:

While my face becomes a mess of snot and tears and dirt from the grass I am ripping out at the roots as I sit there, I throw out one last hook, one last plea to the universe that I am not utterly the victim of my own spectacular illusion-factory.

- But that first time. The kiss. Was that real?

Bugs tick in the afternoon. A flock of Hadidas, those mournful, crying Egyptian Ibisis fly low overhead while he considers. After long moments he speaks.

- Yes.

I tell him I want to go home. And I get up and walk god-knows-where like some sort of mad woman, and he catches up with me and walks me back to the house and sits there quietly with me while I sob and wait for my mother to come and pick me up.

I imagine that as my heart shatters into a thousand tears on that late Sunday afternoon on my way home, he is feeling a vague sense of relief, a sense of anticipation that when he gets back to boarding school he will no longer be carrying the dark image of the besotted Jewish Girl as his inadvertent responsibility.

(Davidow 2016: 151)

Paul

I have many core wounds but one major one is a lack of self-confidence and a propensity to undermine myself and obliterate myself. This arose, I believe, in childhood when my parents were always disappointed in me, wanted me to be someone other than who I was, said things like 'you're not our son,' and led to a lack of self confidence in my abilities, and actions of self-undermining and a need always to prove myself to others, especially my parents. This pattern grew so that I would always try to please others to get their approval, and I could only feel visible or validated if others liked me. The journey to heal this wound has been a lifelong one and one I have not yet written a memoir about. Perhaps that is my next literary task!

As in the above extracts, core wounds are sometimes not obvious and may lie buried in your unconscious for a reason – they may be too traumatic to deal with, so exercise caution in wrestling them to the surface. For example: 'It was the act of making myself small that was the hardest to undo.'

Writing is a lot like therapy, so it's good to be aware that when writing 'what happened' especially when stirring up deep waters, lots of debris may come floating to the surface.

EXERCISE: *Core wounds*

Write a short scene in which the protagonist (you) reveals either through dialogue, action or thought, a 'core wound.' Considering these: abandonment; unrequited love; regret; guilt, write a 200–300-word scene using the examples as a reference to show without telling, one of the above, or any other, core wounds. You do not have to say, *I felt guilty*, or, *I was heartbroken*, but in the sensory detail, your piece will illuminate the sentiment. Show, don't tell.

Shelley

For years I taught the medieval text *Parsifal* by Wolfram von Eschenbach to my Year 11 students. The story is the ultimate grail quest. It was written in the twelfth century about a sixth-century myth – by a man who was an actual twelfth-century knight. Needless to say, the translation from old German is quirky and all the great hero characters are men, whilst female characters languish and either weep or wait for the heroes they love to return or to die – so these elements need to be seen in context – but the most important thing that emerged for me out of years of teaching is that all the characters are archetypes that represent facets of all of us. I can find myself in Parsifal, the naïve young knight who right at the beginning of his journey, has the grail castle in his sight, and yet fails to have the maturity to ask an ailing elderly 'Fisher King', the question that will grant him access to the grail: 'Uncle, what troubles you?' The inability to have empathy or compassion beyond himself sets him on a journey that lasts for hundreds of pages – and is a pertinent metaphor of the journey to self-knowledge and awareness of the impact of a person's actions on others.

Now that you have some core wounds and tragic themes and notes on the hero's journey identified, the longer hero's journey exercise will provide you with an opportunity to reach deeper into yourself, to find, like Parsifal, what your quest might be, to reflect on your journey, and write honestly and without fear about 'what lies beneath'. In this exercise, write as if no one will read it. Give either short or long answers to each question. Give yourself about twenty minutes to complete this.

EXERCISE: *Your ultimate quest*

- What journey/quest are you on?
- What powers do you have?
- What mentor will help you?
- What adversity are you struggling against?
- What/who is your nemesis?
- What threshold experiences do you face?
- Who/what is your 'grail'?

Writing as therapy

In telling our stories, we reframe our narratives. As writing teachers and authors we know the therapeutic power of telling and retelling stories. It has been our experience that focusing on particular themes and going to their depths has helped us see our lives in completely new ways. This focus offers us ways to understand the world and frame the world that sometimes gives the initial event, especially if it was tragic or emotionally impactful, a transformative quality.

If you can see your life as a hero's journey, then the 'dark night of the soul' becomes part of that journey, rather than 'this is how my life is' and the quest for selfhood and understanding the roles other people play in your life can lead to both good story-making, and personal enlightenment.

Shelley

It was at the end of my memoir *Shadow Sisters* (Davidow 2018) where the realization dawned on me that what I'd believed to be a tragic story all my life, might not have been. In fact, this story, told from another perspective, might have been one with a happy ending. My hero's journey which led to tragedy for me was perhaps another character's heroic journey to self-determination and liberation – and it's worth bearing in mind that this could always be the case in any story.

Paul

All my writing is therapy, even when I do not think I am doing therapy. Even my crime novels which I regard as formulaic entertainment explore core wounds, epiphanies, hero's journeys. In *Twelve Days* (Williams 2019), for example, an Agatha Christie locked-room type mystery, the protagonist has a core wound – he has been in love with a particular woman all his life, has nursed his unrequited love for her for many years, and has never been able to get on with his life or love another. At a reunion he finally has to confront this core wound and resolve it once and for all. The reunion is organized by a Christian pastor who wants to bring all his wayward 'sheep' back into the fold. Although not a memoir, this novel deals obliquely with my core wounds – the girl I was in love with whom I wrote about in 'First Kiss', and the religious wound inflicted when I was joined a Christian cult (referred to in the photograph exercise).

Shelley

Years ago, while living in the United States, I was in a writer's group with the inspirational and legendary author Ursula K. Le Guin. For three years I was lucky enough to listen to her responses to my work, to watch her work in the making, and to learn. One of the most important lessons I learned was that you could have a good story, or a good idea for a poem or a great insight. But Ursula Le Guin said and wrote many times, that having a good story, and telling it well, are two completely different things. Every human being, simply by virtue of being alive, has compelling, interesting, tragic and uplifting life events. So why would anyone want to read about your life, or mine? Because they would find there a story that grabbed them and pulled them in – with which they could personally identify. They would be inspired by the writing, the unfolding of the journey. They would feel an affinity with you, the hero of your story, and want to come along with you.

A good memoir – a radical memoir – engages with underlying themes and patterns of a life lived with awareness, pathos, irony even. Perhaps only one theme will be addressed in a single memoir. Radical memoir is as much about process as product. To write a radical memoir you need to be free of constraints – temporal, technical, chronological. Make meaning of your experience in the way you wish to do that. This becomes a metacognitive practice of writing a 'self' into existence – and you may produce a great book as a bonus.

Conclusion

We are hardwired to see life in term of narrative structure. Memoir is the process of capturing that narrative in words, of (re) creating our lives using artistry so that the result is a narrative that draws on every fictional technique to provide a gripping tale. A memoir is not a chronological rambling through every single memory and life event without focus. It is driven by an underlying theme, a primal wound, a hero's journey to selfhood.

4

Memory and neuroscience

Any study about memory draws on many fields – psychology, philosophy, literature, history and of course, neuroscience. The act of remembering is a complex collaboration of interacting elements of cognition involving many areas of the brain. The way we connect our past to our present is a dynamic and non-linear process.

> Current research proves remembering is an unpredictable activity, an inherently creative process of selection, omission, and recreation. Imperfect as it is, however, memory remains central to people's sense of self and identity and, therefore, central to the literature of remembering, memoir.
>
> (O'Rourke 2017: 24)

Shelley

I recently met a woman who was in an accident and lost her memory. She is using a process of writing down people's stories about her to try to re-create/rejig her memories of who she is/was. Every day she writes from a new self that does not remember who her previous self was, to try to send threads into the universe in the hope of rediscovering herself. She collects stories about her past from those who know and love her, and places them in a book. She is in the process of finding herself through narrative. Each piece of her life has to be constructed out of fragments of other people's memories of her, and her life. Her writing is a reconstruction not only of story, but in the most visceral way, of self.

For those of us who have access to our memories, we depend on remembering as we reconstruct our experiences. And most of the time we feel certain that what we remember is true. But therein lies an interesting dichotomy: my truth resides within me. Every act of remembering is an act of recreation. My memory, no matter how good it appears to be, does not provide me with some complete and unchanging hard drive in which the past is located, lying dormant and waiting to be brought to the surface by a smell that takes me back, a song that reminds me of a time. Memories do in fact reside in a complex network of brain structures and processes, but they are tempered at every point of remembering by many different factors. Any two people who experienced the exact same event – the same childhood, for example, can have completely different recollections of that event or childhood, based on what their experience was then, and what it is later, at the moment of recall. My brother and I recently disagreed strongly about a childhood event that both of us were part of that he remembered one way, and I another – and the two memories of what happened were conflicting.

That's not to say that we can't rely on our memories. Of course, we remember, and we can remember very accurately, but memory is not an exact science. So, this is where the potential of the radical memoir lies: as we write to create a memory, we recreate the past, and in so doing, recreate ourselves, then and now – and we can use radical means to do so, because what we are after is a unique truth, a radical truth – yours and mine.

I could start my memoir with an absent narrator. I could use newspaper clippings from South Africa during Apartheid. I could juxtapose those with my childish letters to my grandmother asking her for an umbrella for my birthday, and then add a paragraph from my older self, reflecting on another aspect of my life. The possibilities are as unique and inimitable as a fingerprint.

Personal memory is a limitless resource for story material. Dig deep and find your own way with words to 'paint the pictures' of that deep – staying true to this contract with your reader: this is what it felt like to be that person living through that experience – this is what happened for me.

After writing several memoirs and wrestling with turning my life into art over the past few decades, it's obvious to me that at the heart of the authentic memoir is the necessity to acknowledge that the stories I tell offer one facet of a multi/limitless faceted story – one perspective on an experience (mine), also one story that could have been experienced by a billion others in a billion different ways. That is, if I am writing the singular one-author memoir, as has almost always been the case.

Though we humans are creatures of great similarity in many ways, our identities are singular and inimitable. The hardest disclaimer I wrote was for *Shadow Sisters*. It took me two weeks to distil the 'truth' of how I told 'the truth' or 'my truth' down to this:

> Disclaimer: In this memoir certain names and characteristics of people have been changed to protect their identities, and sometimes timelines have been condensed. Writing a memoir is always a re-imagining, a re-creating, but the author has aimed, nonetheless, for emotional truth.
>
> (Davidow 2018)

Paul

Here is my disclaimer for *Soldier Blue* (2008). I will be discussing this in a later chapter, but here I want to point out how I used Nafisi's quote which is an ironic undermining of any objective truth in memoir grounded in neuroscience.

> DISCLAIMER
> Although this is a memoir and strives to give a 'true' account of the narrator's life, certain events, characters, and characters' names have been changed/blended together to protect identities, and to telescope history into manageable proportions. As Azar Nafisi says in her Author's Note to *Reading Lolita in Tehran*, 'The facts in this story are true insofar as all memories are true'; that is, all history is fictionalized, second-hand, and transmuted by the act of writing into the language of myth, dream and metaphor.
>
> (Williams 2008: iv)

Here's a disclaimer exercise to begin with that may set you free to be authentic in your 'truth-telling'.

EXERCISE: *Disclaimer*

Write a fifty-word disclaimer for the memoir you are writing or will write. You can be humorous, ironic or serious. Write something that sets you free to do what you will be doing. Remember you can and most likely will change this several times once your memoir is complete.

Childhood memories

Shelley

This childhood memory is from *Whisperings in the Blood* (2016) – the unedited version – which was later trimmed to exclude my river metaphor, but which I keep here because I felt this first version was a truer one:

The girl who gives up the violin at eleven thinks the music dies in her, but it doesn't. Like a river that vanishes underground carrying the secret of its source, currents that had their origins in distant times and places sometimes bubble to the surface. They are not immediately recognisable as being part of the hidden river. They emerge in other places, like the ability to speak certain languages without an accent, but she doesn't recognise them. First she is immersed in Afrikaans, the language of the ruling party in South Africa: *Goeie more mense, dis 'n lekker dag vandag.* Then she devours German, which the children learn at school too: *Diese Sprache hört sich sehr vertraut an. Ich spreche fast ohne Akzent.* The German teacher is convinced that the girl must have German parents, but of course she doesn't. She also loves Zulu, the main African language in the Highveld, and taught at school by Mama Gladys, who, as a black Zulu teacher, is an anomaly in the apartheid republic. *Siyabonga Abazali, ufunda isiZulu.* It's the Zulu teacher who takes the girl's small white hands in her dark ones and stares into her eyes, saying, *Woza lapa, Sisi, I will tell you your future: you will travel far away, on planes, and talk to many people in foreign lands.*

(Davidow 2016: unpublished draft)

It is in the perception of events, and not in the events themselves, that the truth of the experience emerges.

Paul

Many people can remember back to when they were as young as three years old, others remember from six, or seven. Some are false memories – our parents told us about an event we had, and we think it is our memory. Often a first memory is associated with a strong emotion or a sensory experience. It may or may not be significant. Here are two of my first memories, documented in *Soldier Blue*. I am not sure if they are real memories as one of them carries with it my mother's guilt as she left me at home with a babysitter while she went to work and it maybe a memory tainted by her later telling me about it.

> My first memory is a stark image of the white bars of my cot, a square, mauve wallpapered room, and a window with sunlight pouring in, beckoning me out of the shadows. I was trapped. However big I felt inside, I was barred in this cot, this box room, by my inability to speak, and that light shaft just outside my reach. I pushed my way out of the cot, so the story goes. I wiggled the bar loose and backwards, nappy first, crashed out into the bare room onto the floor where my parents found me crawling up to the windowsill.
>
> I am also told that I waved goodbye to my mother every morning as she guiltily drove off to work, and, once she had gone, crawled to the chocolate bar on the tea tray which was my reward and her recompense. I remember the black, shiny, puffy arms of the nanny, large Annie, yanking me off to play and sitting in the shade of the Msasa tree, knitting with other loud nannies while we squirmed and squealed as a mass of three-year-olds, bullied and biting and playing in the empty carports of Francis Flats.
>
> (Williams 2008: 7)

I must have been three years old, because I was not at school, and we lived in the government housing provided for teachers at that time. But even at that age, I remember the guilt (I didn't recognize it as guilt then – maybe discomfort, like when someone tells you a fib and looks uneasy) of my parents when they told me that mummy had a job and was going to work in the bank. I remember watching from the living room bay window on the second floor as she drove off in the green Consul and waved. I then knew that as soon as she left, I could go and find the treat she had left me under the doily on the tea tray – always a chocolate bar – and this was, she said, so I would not feel sad. I remember not feeling sad but thinking I ought to. Note the hesitancy in my account. I do not say 'I remember this' but 'I am also told that' because my parents used to tell me this story too, so that the memory and the telling of it become blurred. Even my memory of the cot could be false.

EXERCISE: *First memory*

Using as much sensory imagery as possible, write out your first memory in a paragraph of 300 words. Try to recall what it was like to be that age–what did you hear, smell, taste, feel, think, see? You can write in poetry, play with language, allow the words that convey a sense of that time and place to write themselves. There is no 'correct' way to do this.

When you are done, it might be interesting to consider why this is significant for you, or why you remember this particular event and what significance it has with relation to the rest of your life, or the rest of your memoir.

Hyperthymesia and hypothymesia

Some people remember better than others. If you are gifted with hyperthymesia, you have a superior autobiographical memory and can recall memories others have difficulty with. You may remember details from a very young age, and specific details of events others do not. Hypothymesia, on the other hand, means you have great difficulty remembering past events. It is not necessarily a disadvantage for a memoir writer to have hypothymesia – it just may make the process more creative as you patch together fragments of memories, or like I do, question them.

Shelley

I have kept a diary since I was thirteen. I tend to think I have a good memory because I can tie dates to intense emotional experiences for me. Even so, it is fascinating to me that when I do read back over early diaries, in several instances, my memories are not aligned with my diary entries. For example, I thought that my first boyfriend was the boy I fell in love with when I was thirteen, but when I read back on my diary from that year, I discovered another boy I'd completely forgotten who had a brief supporting role in the drama of my teen years! Granted, he didn't make my heart pound or fill my mind with romantic fantasies – but I discovered in flicking through old pages that I had briefly dated this boy. In my diary, I found the words: 'Yesterday Matthew Kibble tried to kiss me.' I remembered it all as I read it, of course, after that. But, without that note, Matthew Kibble would have been gone from my mind perhaps forever. There are the memories that we capture by writing, and the ones that sit there dormant, sleeping in the cracks, which can be brought to light by certain experiences or by someone else sending us a reminder.

I recently sat at a green retro table from the 1970s at a funky cafe in remote Queensland in Australia. I looked at the strange green melamine table covering and suddenly remembered that we'd had such a table when I was about a year old. My mother was with me and I was able to ask her whether we'd had a yellow version of the same table. Yes, she said, exactly.

I would not have accessed that memory, had we not stopped at that little tea place somewhere between Childers and Agnes Water in Queensland, Australia.

So how then do we dig deep and find memories long forgotten?

Just as the photograph exercise can elicit emotional memory, so, too, can this game: *what did you eat for breakfast on August 25, 2003?*

By a process of elimination, you can figure out where you were, whom you were with, what you were doing, and at least come close to remembering what you might have had for breakfast on that day.

Or you can track more broadly the emotional territory of a particular year or month. For example, I know that I was in Germany in a particular year in September because that was the time I caught chickenpox and it was during the school break when the weather was getting colder and the days were getting shorter. I also remember the feeling when my mother brought my baby brother home from the hospital, and he had an egghead and I thought he wasn't as cute as I expected him to be – I was three and a half. Emotional states, smells, sights, sounds, can take us back to early experiences.

Paul

When I published *Soldier Blue*, readers would often ask me how I remembered so many details of my childhood. I told them that I exercised my memory in various ways (see below) and also did some research in order to jog my memory. I did archival research, read newspapers of the time, looked at photos, interviewed family members and friends in order to get an accurate picture of the fragments of memories I had lodged in my brain. It is amazing how much you can remember when you have prompts!

Recalling memories

It is all in there somewhere. Or is it? We often like to think of the brain as some gigantic computer and hard drive that contains all the imagery files of every event that you ever experienced, and you just need to access that RAM memory to find it again. But we are biological, emotional and psycho-spiritual entities with the capacity to imagine and create, and there is much that takes place that is part of our experience of being that can't be adequately squashed into a computerized metaphor.

From a neuroscientific perspective, there are three areas of the brain involved in memory: the hippocampus, the neo-cortex and the amygdala. The Hippocampus is where memories are formed and indexed for later access. These are 'episodic' or 'autobiographical' memories from specific events in our lives. The neocortex is responsible for sensory perception, motor commands, spatial reasoning and language, and memories stored in the hippocampus are transferred to the neocortex (during sleep) during which time we 'rehearse' new experiences and accumulate knowledge. The amygdala is where emotional significance is given to memories. These are the memories we remember the most. The interaction of the three parts of the brain – the amygdala, hippocampus and neocortex – helps create stable memories that can be retained for long periods of time and can be accessed through mnemonic devices. If these areas of the brain are damaged, our memories are damaged or erased, or we can't access them – but there are still areas of great mystery where sometimes, the ineffable human overcomes even the greatest odds – like the musician who, after a long time in a coma, came to consciousness and could only remember up to seven minutes of his life. Every seven minutes, he thought he had just woken from a coma, and yet as a pianist and musician, he was still able to learn and retain new and complex pieces and play them (Sacks 2007).

Memory retrieval happens when we revisit the nerve pathways that were created when the memories were first stored and encoded.

We can recall memories in three ways – what is called 'free recall', randomly accessed in any order, 'cued recall' where some cue or guide helps us to retrieve specific memories linked to the cue, such as ones associated with other memories, or paired with others, and 'serial recall' where events are remembered in the order of their chronological occurrence. Short-term memories are easier to recall than long-term memories – unless you have lost your memory, in which case, it depends on the damage. With dementia, the hippocampus, located in the temporal lobe, is often the area first damaged – and is the one responsible for creating new memories (Dementia Care Central 2021: np).

EXERCISE: *Cued recall*

Here is a memory recall exercise based on the previous discussion. **Tuesday 29 October 2005, 3 pm.**

Write for six minutes about that day, that time, trying to recreate as closely as possible a memory of that afternoon. To start off, consider what you were doing that year. Where did you live? What work were you doing? Who was in your life? What did you usually do on Tuesday afternoons? What was the weather like usually? Where you were in October?

You may be able to 'remember' now. You may need to check the weather for that day, your school schedule, your job calendar. You may also need to check facts about that day, ask friends, family, and you could probably cheat and look back on social media, whatever form of it existed back then.

Most people can remember significant events as the memories are etched into their brains via heightened emotional experiences. For example, most people who were old enough will remember exactly what they were doing at 9 am 2001 when the Twin Towers were hit on September 11th.

EXERCISE: *Free recall*

Write without stopping for five minutes: write about a song, a smell, a taste or an image that triggers an emotional recollection of a particular time and place in the past. For example, the smell of briny sea air on a windy beach day.

False memories

It is possible too that when we think we remember, we are in fact recalling false memories. Often beliefs interfere in our retrieval of data, and post-event information can distort or alter memories. Newer memories may also be layered on top of old memories, confusing them. Our memory files become corrupt and as we get older, we seem to forget things more and more. We have to practise and exercise memory recall. Even the wording of a question we use when trying to retrieve a memory may change the information. We may really believe we are remembering something accurately when we are not. How do we verify? It is always good to keep a journal of our emotional life, not just record events in a list-like fashion but write down our thoughts and insights about events. In this way we can always go back and check if our memories are accurate.

Paul

Soldier Blue was possible because I kept a journal of my army years, and much of the memoir which readers dispute as being too 'far-fetched' is literally factual, documented in my journal entries with dates and minute-by-minute written records and facts to back it up. Sometimes when I re-read that memoir, I do not believe what actually happened, and have to go back to the original records to check – yes, it did happen.

Memories can also be distorted by repetition: the more we tell them, the more they change. But if we go deeper enough inside ourselves, we can always find a true memory, usually accessed by a deep emotion. My first memories of my mother leaving for work every day are detailed and imbued with a deep emotion. In spite of the hesitancy in my account ('I am also told that'), I do remember the feeling, the experience, the phenomenological, sensory, tactile sense of being at that moment. The first memory of the cot could be false, but I can still remember the smells, texture of the blanket, the embodiment of that moment in the cot, and the urge to escape.

Memory is story

As discussed, memory retrieval is not simply getting fixed data that is stored somewhere, like a file we can access and read. In *Remapping Your Mind: The Neuroscience of Self-Transformation through Story* Lewis Mehl-Madrona suggests that memories are not static. They are changed and re-written depending on where we stand in the present. British neuroscientist Mark Turner also maintains that human mental functioning has its basis in story. We access memory not as a list or series of facts, but in narrative form. And Bruner concurs: 'We organize our experience and our memory of human happenings mainly in the form of narrative' (Bruner 1991: 4). And like all narrative, memory is influenced by present context: memories are reborn and remade in the present, just a narrative is a retrospective story told by a narrator in the present who shapes that past material. If we think about that photo written about in Chapter 1, it is a piece of data around which memories of the day and time and place are reconstructed. The memory is 'retrieved' but reinterpreted depending on when and in which context it is recalled. The data is slotted into a narrative story to provide context. The process of recall is always contextual and shaped by story. Memory is not written down and captured unproblematically, but rather is emotive, sensory and associative. The recalling and rewriting of specific moments, like writing our core wounds, can transform a traumatic experience for the writer, rewrite it and make a new reality out of it, as Mehl-Madrona indicates.

Shelley

Trauma and healing through narrative

Trauma often plays a significant part in the reason we are drawn to writing memoir. This is an experience I know for myself: my autobiographical novel *Freefalling* was precipitated by the death of a friend; *The Eye of the Moon* (2008) was precipitated by heartbreak; *Whisperings in the Blood* (2016) was the result of opening a box of inherited letters from my dead grandmother and feeling my family's past and their history of broken dreams rush over me like a tidal wave. The memoir writer's job, we might believe, is to tell a good story. But something happens along the way. Our writing can also be a kind of re-making of self. Our memories are reconstructed and sometimes, perhaps transformed.

Narrative therapy is a technique that has been used for decades in order to anchor people's experience, to help them make sense of their trauma by contextualizing it, allowing people to change and re-create scenarios that eventuate in their healing (Madagan 2011), but even if this is not the aim of the memoir-writer, the crafting of a memoir can result in the personal transformation of the writer.

I'm interested in the degree to which our own writing around our wounds, our traumas and reactions to those, inform the memoir-writer's process. In the previous chapter on the Hero's Journey, we discussed an archetypal trajectory as inherent in every memoir: as we write, we set out to solve a problem. Sometimes, the actual writing and constructing of this journey give us an unexpected solution, some sort of solace or remedy that comes as a result of the crafting of lived experience into an art form.

When we write about trauma, we are in risky territory. It can be too painful to process, and I have at least a handful of friends who began memoirs only to abandon them because the 'debris' they unearthed was too much to bear.

There is also a literary risk: writing about our heartaches can become sentimental, can appear self-indulgent and might then be relegated to the pile of 'poor me' or 'misery memoirs' that dump misery on the reader, point fingers of blame, and have the effect of simply 'getting it off the writer's chest'.

To write about trauma well, a writer needs craft and skill and must have a literary and artistic goal. The crafting and patchworking and bowerbirding that the radical memoir enables are exciting. It may take the courage to break with traditional expectations, to experiment with form to eventuate a memoir that transforms both writer and reader.

An example of transformational memoir-writing can be found in the Australian collaborative memoir *Mothertongues* (2022) by authors and mothers Ceridwen Dovey and Eliza Bell, whose genre-defying work draws on theatre of the absurd, poetry, lists and dialogue to convey the heartbreak, chaos and emotion of young motherhood. Even if it rambles and goes 'off-course', I have to applaud the risk taken, the road travelled. The way this form allows the writers to outrun self-pity and sentimentality was exceptional. The book defies traditional narrative conventions, sometimes displacing the reader, as the writers seek to show the visceral loss of cohesion that happens in the lives of new mothers. The two authors embrace, sometimes to confusing effect, the dissonance many women experience as mothers. With two voices, the raw and emotional account of mothering is amplified through their eclectic use of a range of literary forms. The authors have even gone multimedia and recorded the songs written so readers can go to their website and download them. To me this collaborative, expansive work is a prime example of the radical memoir: it is an expressionist, post-modern capturing of 'real life' and the form shedding light on the non-linear. This kind of narrative allows for both the writers and readers to confront the experiences of love and trauma amidst chaos.

The other radical memoir that took eight years to write and straddles the genres of memoir, biography and autobiography, as well as investigative journalism, whilst deftly keeping the author's own life almost entirely invisible is Lisa Taddeo's *Three Women* (2019). Taddeo's own story, told in the first person about her mother walking to work in Italy followed by a masturbating man is on the margins or the stories of three other women, each told in a unique and different voice. Maggie's story, for example, is told in the second person – a position which grabs the reader by the scruff of her neck and compels her to become the character. Sloane's and Lina's stories are in the third person, so there is the awareness of Taddeo as reporter, though the details are so intimate we know the author is much closer than a mere recorder of 'what happened'. The book is made up of the result of thousands of hours of interviews, court documents and conversations with the protagonists over almost a decade. At the end, we learn with horror that the teacher, Aaron Knodel who had sex with Maggie when she was his pupil at school has been found innocent of abuse and is back teaching high school girls. The book is gut-turning in its raw exposure of women's lives. Importantly, the craft is extraordinary:

> Six years ago, you were smaller, and he loved your little hands. Back then, his own hands fluttered inside you. A lot has changed. Your father is dead. In August, he slit his wrists in a nearby cemetery. You used to talk to him about your dad, about the problems with your parents. He knew how one would go to pick up the other from a bar. Both drunk, but one worse than the other. Now you feel he'd understand, how you are worried about rain

pattering on the ground above your dad. Is he getting wet down there, and wondering why you have left him in the cold, bucketing dark? Doesn't death supersede all this other bullshit, even the cops and the lawyers? Isn't it, somehow, somewhere, still just the two of you?

(Taddeo 2019: 2)

In this story, we never find out what event in Taddeo's own life (not in her mother's) propelled the writer to tell these women's stories. Perhaps dealing with other women's issues heals her own buried trauma – readers will never know. What is clear is that there is nothing sentimental or 'poor me' or 'poor her' about this story. And this is because the finely crafted narrative that pushes the work into an art form beyond the facts of the story.

For many memoir writers, working creatively on sculpting a narrative offers some healing of their own wounds and traumas.

Our brains are excited by the new, the non-cliched images that explode when we are confronted with the unfamiliar, the unusual – and in this experience, emotional transportation happens, and we may, as readers, be changed. But the writer too must have gone through a process to craft these words just so – to distil emotional experience into just the right words, and in doing this, perhaps the writer's past is healed to some degree. I found myself emotionally transported, aligned, holding my breath as I read this paragraph in which Hisham Mater discusses grief and death in *The Return*:

Grief is not a whodunnit story, or a puzzle to solve, but an active and vibrant exercise. It is hard, honest work. It can break your back. It is part of one's initiation into death and – I don't know why, I have no way of justifying it- it is a hopeful part at that. What is extraordinary is that, given everything that has happened, the natural alignment of the heart remains towards the light … declarative statements such as 'He is dead' are not precise. My father is both dead and alive. I do not have a grammar for him. He is in the past, present and future.

(Matar 2016: 167)

A radical memoir has the capacity to be transformative for both reader and writer.

Paul

Writing the memoir as healing process

There is a long tradition of the memoir as self-therapy where the memoirist writes a 'confession' in order to heal themselves of issues they are grappling with. 'Confession' has a religious connotation, and this metaphor may be one that is useful for you: you write to confess your 'sins' or your traumas or whatever is bothering you, and you confess not to a priest or to God but to yourself, or to the world. Saint Augustine's *Confessions* (CE 397–400) was perhaps the first memoir where the writer sought to reconstruct his soul that he said was in ruins. Julian of Norwich, Teresa of Avila and Therese of Lisieux wrote similar confessional memoirs in order to heal their souls through self-knowledge.

We write to deal with past trauma, to confront something that haunts us and which we want to process. But if memory is a treasure trove, it is also a minefield. *Soldier Blue* was an exercise for me of picking my way back through that minefield and rescuing myself. Dealing with trauma by writing about it alone may be manageable for some, but for others it may be advisable to work with a therapist. I tackled my past trauma alone and only when I was ready – it took me twenty years before I could go back into some of the places I have been, but I confronted them head on and felt a sense of catharsis for doing so, so much so that the elements of PTSD I was experiencing disappeared. No more nightmares about the war and Major Maddox once they were out in print form. It took honesty and painful self-recognition to go to some of those places and it is as if I had erased the pain of the past and replaced it with a story. I had overwritten my life with a fiction. I had also externalized my trauma and placed it between the covers of a book. Writing memoir is a dangerous form of therapy because it demands that you open those wounds, dig into those buried traumas, examine your core wound and face it head on. But writing memoir is a well-researched means of healing and overall improvement in psychological and physical health. Rebecca M. Painter in 'Healing Personal History: Memoirs of Trauma and Transcendence' suggests that writing memoir demands 'fully mindful attention as the medium of creative resolution and the transformation of individual consciousness to new levels of personal growth and healing' (Painter 2009: 1).

In the same article, David Grossman, one of Israel's pre-eminent novelists and thinkers, maintains that writing memoir is 'a means of transcending the enslavement of degrading personal memories', a form of psychotherapy:

> Why we seek to plumb our deepest subliminal empirical psyche in psychoanalysis … and why we always talk about our past as well as that of our families and friends: we are bringing all these things up from the dark spheres of our psyche into the luminosity of the significant word.
>
> (Painter 2009: 1)

Shelley

Dreams

Dreams are the stories that we tell ourselves when we are completely devoid of control, in an unconscious state – and it is this brain state that shows us how profoundly we are narrative creatures. Stories, metaphors, archetypes abound. We share so many fears, desires, hopes as narrative humans. We are chased, rescued, helped, attacked. We confront kind dream-people and menacing ones. Animal totems appear. We do battle with serpents and our teeth fall out. Planes drop out of the sky. An injured bird needs help. And sometimes, we learn to control the narrative while in this altered state. During lucid dreaming (a heightened state during REM sleep which can be induced through specific practices), the dreamer goes through phases of cognition in order to establish in the unconscious state that the dream is in fact a dream, and then to assume first-person protagonist position to influence the narrative (Stumbrys, Erlacher, Schädlich & Schredl 2012) – and the beauty of this is that I as the dreamer, confront themes, creatures and experiences thrown up by my deepest subconscious, and then am compelled to make, change, direct a story. Story is indeed everything. It shapes us and we shape ourselves through narratives. Our brains are primed for story making and we can be the powerless subjects of powerful dreams or learn to control how the narrative evolves.

On occasion, I've had lucid dreams, where I've been able to become aware of my dream and control the narrative, but always for me, only to a point. Recently, I dreamt I was riding a scooter at breakneck speed through an Italian village. The village opened up into a field and the scooter went faster and faster, heading towards a drop that I could see opened into a valley far below. As the speed picked up insanely, I realized that this could not possibly be happening in real life. I worked out, thought by thought, that this was a dream. As soon as I realized that, I allowed the dream to continue, much as you would if you were catching a wave as a bodysurfer. I let it pick me up, but I guided it. As the scooter reached the edge of the field that fell away into a steep escarpment, I made myself fly. I felt exhilarated. I felt the wind in my hair. I congratulated myself on achieving full flight without any prior dream-flying-lessons. In the dream I thought that this level of lucid control would only be possible after first doing some low, slow learner-flying, but here I was, high and fast over green hills. In that moment I realized I could do anything I wanted in the whole universe. So I flew to Cape Town and landed the scooter outside the house of my old teacher, whom I loved, who died seventeen years ago. She was at her house, dressed in white, and so happy to see me. She invited me in but apologized for not having any food to offer me, because she hadn't been expecting me. I said I really didn't need anything to eat – seeing her was enough. I became aware that I was now almost her age – that we were of the same generation – and we sat down and talked about our children, how they were. At this point, I was aware that I was beginning to wake up. I didn't want her to think me rude if I vanished, so I quickly said goodbye, went out to the scooter and woke up. I lay in my bed, stunned for a few minutes. Yes, I had guided the story, but it had also written itself. Some elements were in my control, others completely random, as if provided by a Great Writer – some Dream Co-ordinator – the profoundly mysterious narrative-driven subconscious.

The point of this? To highlight how profoundly our dreams demonstrate that we are innately story makers: in this mythical, highly metaphorical landscape, symbolism and archetypes play out against the backdrop of fears, hopes and dreams. Even when we think we're writing fiction, we are writing parts of ourselves and experiences into the story. In memoir, the emotional territory of our lives is the backdrop. It's then up to me, up to you, as writers to allow the metaphors and symbols of your hero's journey, your unique theme to emerge as you craft and re-craft your life as a potent story that others will find compelling.

EXERCISE: *Multi-sensory scene building using dreams*

Write a descriptive paragraph (300–500 words) that brings a sensory experience from a dream to life. Focus on sight, smell, touch, sound, taste – all or any of them. Can you re-create the details, but also the corresponding emotion? Show the impact of that experience/dream (which could be a dream from long ago) and how it inscribed itself into your memory.

Paul

What fascinates me about dreams is that they are narratives that use the same language we use in fiction – metaphor, symbolism, allegory – and they use narrative to sort out our daytime events, sifting through the data and processing it. If anything is too disturbing for our conscious minds to handle, they disguise it in metaphor so that we can still process the trauma. I am simplifying, but this is what dreams do, and I make a point of trying to remember my dreams and interpreting them. Memoir then, if it is to tell our story, should account for our unconscious selves as well, and we should allow that dark matter of our universe to speak too.

One of my favourite memoir titles is Vladimir Nabokov's *Speak, Memory!* (1951). To write memoir is to call to your deeper self, the stories lurking in those hidden, forgotten places, and invoke them to 'speak!' Nabokov's autobiographic memoir consists of essays, and contains perhaps the best opening line ever to begin a memoir: 'The cradle rocks above an abyss, and common sense tells us that our existence is but a brief crack of light between two eternities of darkness' (Nabokov 1951:1).

Conclusion

Exercises in memory recall and reconstruction focus on using these emotive, sensory and associative techniques to build a sense of place, time and experience. In this way, the memoir writer is doing the same as the fiction writer, constructing a rich, multi-layered world into which a reader might step. The characters within this world are real, but they are constructed in much the same way as fictional characters would be. Sometimes this may eventuate in a transformative process for the writer. Our interpretations of our lives, our encounters with our own deep metaphors through contemplation, dreams and the act of writing are the raw material out of which a memoir evolves.

5

The art of turning real people into characters

Shelley

In memoir, we have to turn the real people in our lives into characters in a story. I have found this one of the most difficult parts of writing memoir. It's a very rare person who remembers exactly what was said and when and how and can depict a person accurately in their memoir. Creating characters, their dialogue and conversations that are both authentic and engaging for a reader is a challenge on many fronts. To be fair, we do often recall exactly what was said, by whom and in which manner, but much of what memoir writers do is *re-creation.* Did I really say that to my brother on that rainy night when we were four and seven? Perhaps. Could he have a different memory of the same event? Perhaps. What if he becomes a character in my story, and my version of him overwrites his own experience of his own life – and my book is published and that is the version of him that goes out to the world?

We are entering the complex realm of ethics. I can't say anything comfortable about the dynamic process of turning the people in your life into characters. You have to write your story in the way that you want to write it, and your characters speak and move as you decide, based on your sense of 'what really happened'. This is exciting and problematic and never stops being both.

When I wrote *Whisperings in the Blood,* a biographical memoir and therefore fraught with the issues of writing other characters, I based the book on hundreds of letters written to my grandmother from 1938 until about 1983 that I had found. I also had her 1938–41 diary. I had her 'voice'. I created scenes in the book, some of which used her words in her diary and some of which drew on the words in the letters written to her by friends to create a sense of who she was (she used the vernacular of her time, so she took 'snaps' not photos, movies were 'pictures', things were 'swell', and exclamations of surprise were 'oh my'). But the context had to be recreated entirely. I had to draw on all my powers as a fiction writer to create her, her words and her experiences as authentic elements in my story. In so doing, I created what I hoped would be a worthy narrative. I honoured her, her life, her journey, her struggles. But when I was finished, I looked at the box of letters, at her diary entries, and felt a sense of having done something irrevocable: was it possible that I had literally 'written over' her life, in my attempt to 'preserve' and treasure her? I don't know. Here's an extract from my book, a recreation of a scene based closely on a letter written to my gran by her best friend Gertrude:

The hot summer evenings go on forever. Gert and Bert walk arm in arm under the trees.

-*Berty, imagine, fifty years from now, these trees will be huge. These sticks will turn into oaks and line the walkway with shade.*

-*And we'll be old.*

-*Not that old. We'll probably be long married, with kids, oh my. And we'll be able to bring them here and walk them down a long shady avenue.*

-*Yeah.*

-*What do you want to be, Berty?*

-*Oh, I don't know. Happy, I guess.*

-*Don't you want to be married, and have a swell home, a handsome husband, and great friends? I do.*

-*Honestly I have no idea what will make me happy.*

-*You could be a star in the pictures, you're that pretty. Just a bit thin if I might say.*

-*You might not!*

-*Well, I just did!*

-*I like these trees, Gert. They'll be like our ghosts. Long after we leave, they'll be here, whispering our secrets to future generations.*

-Oh, promise me we'll always, always be friends. I just couldn't stand it if we weren't.

-Of course we will!

-I reck'n we should live in the same neighbourhood so we can celebrate Shabbos and Channukah and Pesach and everything together. Like family. I do hate the idea of being far away from you.

(Davidow 2016: 20)

EXERCISE: *Creating Characters out of people you know*

Write a scene from your life (300 words) and at the centre of this, create a piece of dialogue between you and one of your 'characters' or between people you know. Describe the setting, and the characters with brief 'brushstrokes'. Allow the dialogue to reveal who these people are. Somewhere in the dialogue, ensure you place a statement or some words that you are sure you actually said/heard. Build the interaction around that.

Paul

An old saying attributed to Socrates, but used in my youth group by our leader whenever we were tempted to scandal or gossip about others, was this: before you say anything about another person, you must ask yourself three questions: – *is it truthful, is it necessary and is it kind?* This normally squashed any gossip (which was normally none of the above). But what if we write about others in our memoirs? Surely we cannot just give rosy depictions of people, or leave them out if our portraits are less than flattering? Surely we have a duty to speak truth and to be honest about our lives? Inevitably someone will not like what we write about them. And even if what we write is flattering, it may not be what they themselves remember, or want to remember, or want written about them.

Of course we should play fair and not write vindictively to air a grievance or settle a score. Try to avoid writing the 'misery memoir' or the 'vengeance memoir' where you use your space and power to even scores or slander some enemy or show how hard done by you were. To be fair, the misery memoir is a respectable literary genre that focuses on (usually childhood) trauma and abuse, and has been immensely popular. The seminal 'misery memoir' is Dave Pelzer's *A Child Called It* (1995) reveals a horrific abusive childhood at the hand of his mother. But it is an easy bad habit to fall into and the 'poor, poor, pitiful me' victim theme can sometimes put readers off, especially if the claims and the way other characters are portrayed are accusatory.

Some misery memoirs read like vendettas, for example, CBS's Katie Couric's memoir *Going There* (2021). The book attacks her former employees and colleagues with a venom that makes the reader squirm: 'every short chapter comes across like a rabbit punch aimed at the kidneys of one former acquaintance after another' comments a reviewer (Justin 2021).

The problem with writing the personal vendetta memoir is that the writer often comes off badly in such books, and attempts to gain sympathy or get readers 'on side' can backfire. People can sue us for libel if they feel their character has been tarnished. Memoir demands careful consideration of how writers write about others.

So how does a writer write about people in their lives honestly without offending them? One option is to show the people involved what's been written about them and ask them if they are happy to have themselves written about in this way. Consent, however, is not always possible, or even desirable, and may become complicated if they want a say in how they are written about or disagree with the writer's perception of events. Writers of memoir are compelled to do a cost/benefit analysis and decide on how much other people's wishes should be taken into account. Each story is unique and has different demands.

EXERCISE: *Remember this*

With a family member or friend, discuss incidents in the past that you both remember, involving the two of you. Select one incident. Each person should write a 300–500-word paragraph that captures what happened and describes each person from the other's point of view. Share with each other and discuss. What are the discrepancies?

It is never so simple as 'writing about others' as if we were taking photos of them – our portrayal of others is constructed – and can never be objective. It is always the best defence to claim subjectivity, and this may save you (and others) a lot of grief. Admit that this is your subjective take on them, and how you remembered things, to tell 'your' truth about how you experienced them. Admit that it may be inaccurate, wrong, unfair, but this is how you saw them.

I could not show my memoir *Soldier Blue* to my family, because I decided to be honest – maybe too honest – about my feelings about them. I called my parents naïve, my uncle myopic, my friends betrayers. I was struggling to understand myself in relation to them and was being honest as a method to try to understand myself in relation to them.

> My parents were neither racist colonisers, rabid capitalists, nor ranting missionaries. They had no business in Africa, and were, I now sadly conclude, simply naïve. But by committing themselves to settling there, Africa became their problem, and mine. And Africa did not tolerate naiveté … I have to admire them for bravely tearing the umbilical cord of family tradition. No Williams had ever set foot out of England before, and most of them had never ventured out of Norwich. If Norwich was good enough for my grandfather, my uncle said, it was good enough for him.
>
> (Williams 2008: 11)

My fears were unfounded – some of family did read the memoir and did not complain at all about the way I depicted them. On the contrary, they praised the book's honesty. I hoped that I had fairly described the people in my life, but I wrote mercilessly. I was critical of bullies at school, those who had hurt me or betrayed me, all the while being aware and hopefully communicating to my readers that this was a subjective, personal account by a naïve narrator. And to be fair I was brutally honest about myself too, and perhaps that is what redeemed the book for others who I portrayed 'warts and all'.

I felt it was necessary, for example, to describe in detail the bullying commander in the army who made my life hell. I pulled no punches. But I did change his name to protect him. I also did, to be fair, give him a human side, so that readers could see a three-dimensional character, one I was striving to portray as accurately as possible.

> Even Major Madox, if he is still alive, would smile. Stooped, haggard, in the prison of civilian clothes, shuffling in dismay at being left abandoned in his old age in the Africa he tried so hard to prevent, he'd clutch my arm. Doc! Doc! You wanted us to lay down our arms and give up. You wanted the comrades to take over the villages, the ttl's, the country. You wanted them to murder, maim, kill their own people. Well, here you are. This is what you wanted. Are you happy now? Was I right or was I wrong?
>
> (Williams 2008: 393)

I wanted to portray how I felt as an eighteen-year-old, acquiescent, insecure army recruit in the power of a man I regard now as mentally ill, delusional and dangerous. I may have been unfair and biased in my portrayal of him, and he may have disputed my portrayal – some would say caricature – of him, but I felt and still feel that this reflects my accurate emotional state at the time.

I did get backlash from people who said I was being unfair, inaccurate about my depictions of them in the book. Some were deeply offended, others confirmed my views, even recognizing characters I had thought I had cleverly disguised. I even think I inadvertently offended an old English teacher whom I admired by quoting her directly and using her real name. 'Enter Miss Botha, our English teacher, who believed that literature could save the world. ... Literature is life, boys; literature is life' (Williams 2008: 74). I meant it to be a compliment, but in her correspondence with me after she read the memoir, I got the feeling she took it as mockery.

The lesson is clear: you will never know how people respond to your portrayals of them in your memoir so, on the one hand, be very careful how you portray 'real' people, but, on the other, be honest and tell the truth about them as unflinchingly as you tell the truth about your own life.

The radical concept in this chapter is the most obvious notion that the supposedly 'real' people we write about in our memoirs, however much we try to be accurate, are avatars, creative, subjective reflections, representations. Memoirs are perhaps mistakenly read as journalistic accounts. They are not.

They are constructed creative narratives, impressionist paintings rather than photographs fashioned by words and imagination in place of physical colour and light, on paper.

Memoir as the erasure of others

Memoir, we accept, is revelatory. It uncovers and reveals what lies beneath – namely, the truth of the writer's life. In memoir, the 'reader/writer contract' is premised on the understanding that 'this really happened'. Even if we understand that memoir does not seek to represent exactly what was done on this day at this time, the way a journalistic or autobiographical account of a life might strive to do, the reader of a memoir assumes that the writer strives for emotional 'truth' and this equally applies to the truth of others.

In the critically reflective piece below on *Shadow Sisters*, the uncomfortable question arises: what if memoir, in its making, becomes a masking, an over-writing, in a sense an obliteration of the people we write into our pages – our families, friends, lovers? What if, by writing a story that we believe is revelatory, that we believe tells the truth about our lives, we function as erasers? What if our words, given primacy because they are the ones that get published, read, disseminated, wipe out the voices, the stories, the very agency of the people close to us who have by necessity become characters in our life-stories?

Shelley

It took me decades to come to a place where I could write about my life growing up in South Africa during Apartheid with an unofficially adopted black sister – at a time when it was regarded as criminal for Black and white people to live under one roof as a family. The writing of my memoir *Shadow Sisters* was tricky because it was as much other people's stories as it was my own. As I wrestled with the ethics of telling a story that was so intricately also another person's story, I had to make difficult choices. I got as much input as I could. I shared the manuscript with those I could share with.

I took some of the advice, but not all. In critical situations, I could not get input and I had to decide – do I abandon this project, or do I tell this story that lives under my skin? I did the best I could. I couldn't not tell this story, but I was aware that there could be emotional fall-out. I just didn't see it coming from where it did: when my mother read *Shadow Sisters* after it was published in 2018, she said this. 'It's beautiful.' I was relieved. I'd tried to ensure emotional fidelity to my experience of her, to her work, her story. 'But,' she said, 'it made me feel strange. As though I somehow lost agency in my own life.'

I was stunned. How could I not have anticipated this? Could this have been avoided? Would this go on now forever since that book was now out, and that process would continue to play itself out? 'Thanks,' I said. 'I have no idea what to do about that.'

I still don't know what to do about that.

This is the territory of memoir: it's risky. There is no single truth, and no way to ensure fairness, equity, accurate representation of everyone's voice, interests, perceptions.

Lives are tangled and lived by many people, together; a writer can never just tell their own story. Necessarily, we tell the stories of others. We take licence. We portray them so that they are true to our emotional experience of them. But then that's the story that goes out there, gets read. My mother was approached sometimes by people who did not know her who said, 'Oh, I read Shelley's book and I feel I know you.'

She was surprised. Eventually she told these people that what they knew was my picture of her.

There is a complex and unavoidable dichotomy that plays out as we write about others' lives. Since I am the writer whose work is being published, it is my version of events, my version of the people in my family that gets projected out into the world, and it's not as though every person in the narrative has an equal right of response, because to have that, each person would have to write, and have published, their version of the story, and every person who read my version, would have to read theirs, and only then would we be able to say that there is equity in terms of having the right to share and create a shared history/story. And of course that's never going to happen. So, all I can do is acknowledge that what I am presenting is my version of my experience – and I understand now profoundly that in writing to 'reveal' the truth, I am simultaneously writing over the 'truth', remaking it according to my own disposition and recollection.

Likewise, in my biographical memoir *Whisperings in the Blood*, I have recreated the lives of my great grandfather, my grandmother, my father and the people around them – I have built them up out of their written words, their letters and telegrams and photographs. I have, as a narrative creature, created a story and they are characters in it, and it's possible that while in many ways I've paid homage to them, to their lives, brought my beloved ancestors to life and made it possible for others to read those lives and appreciate them – there is no doubt that I have also erased them, written over them. I have left my version of their experiences as the last word.

That, in and of itself, is a burden.

Who am I to have the last say on the lives of all those people?

But without my stories about them, who would even know that, for example, my ancestors lived, and loved and lost? And who would care?

So yes, it's a burden. And I don't say this lightly. I say it because it's important to know that when you set out to write your truth, you are also making at the very least a partial fiction out of someone else's lived experience. There is definitely a sense of unease in me about that – but I have no idea what to do except live in the discomfort and understand that as the writer, I am not the guardian of family truth – only of my own truth.

Writing memoir is an art as much as writing a work of fiction or poetry is, in the sense that our words are always a proxy: they represent our thoughts, feelings, emotional landscapes, ideas – and they provide what we hope to be access to these imaginative landscapes and the people within them. Whilst our words can only ever assist readers in the imagining of the worlds and characters we make, we measure and value a literary work in essence, by how powerfully those words are able to emotionally transport a reader. If we use our words well and they do what we mean them to do, they vanish. A reader may be sitting on a chair next to a window, a fire, or lying on a beach, but really, they are somewhere else – walking with the writer through a childhood street, popping Jacaranda blossoms under their feet.

So much of the power of words to create/annihilate lies in the spaces between.

As a memoir-writer, I have wrestled with words to make them convey what it was 'really like'. How did it feel? What was the emotional impact? But do we write over the ones we love? Is it my right to write this, I ask, as I described, based on what my sister told me, because she was there, she saw it, how my father was arrested by an Afrikaans policemen, who said, 'now we will teach you Jews a lesson', how my dad was thrown into jail, accused of fraud, and all this the night before he was supposed to immigrate to Canada?

I was down the road in an apartment. I didn't see this event. I heard about it. I spoke to my stepmom and dad afterwards.

I lived through how the case against him was dropped, and how he lost his Canadian residence as did we, and our lives all changed from that moment on. When I wrote this out, I was trying to convey the raw fear and devastation of the night – how I tried to sleep knowing that my gentle father was somewhere in Johannesburg in a prison cell, this pharmacist who had never harmed anyone and who was the kindest of men. But was it my right to write it? I wasn't the one in prison. I wasn't there when he was arrested. I wonder now, have I subsumed/consumed that and created an image of it that diminishes the experience of the people close to me? In my darkest moments I feel as a memoir writer like a literary cannibal – am I at some level consuming the people in my life and history, leaving behind in the public sphere, avatars of the people in my life that I have constructed?

The act of remembering is always an act of recreation. I stand alone in my history and I tell other people's stories, pulling them into my art in a way that may not, let's face it, be beneficial to them or even desired by them even though it serves my purpose of turning my life into art. And yet I write without stopping into that ethical and paradoxical place where I recreate real people and, in the process, perhaps diminish their voices, their agency in a world in which my version of events takes precedence. The next evolution, then, requires something radical, which is what we will discuss in the chapter on collective memoir, which has exciting potential for the future because it allows for more than one voice and breaks the singularity of one person's perspective.

Meanwhile, I continue to wonder after each memoir: what have I done? And can it be undone? And should it be undone? Due to the risks, the potential for erasures, the contradictions, should I not tell my story?

With each memoir I have had to decide: do I push ahead anyway? What matters most? I've found a way around this in some instances by changing names, personal details and settings to such a degree that the real person is not only left alone, but I have created a fictional character in their place.

The thick line then, between fiction and non-fiction grows so thin it's almost a strand of gossamer. The contract that 'this really happened' is still there, but there are not only disguised, but substitute characters in this true story, to protect identities.

I try to deal with that in disclaimers. Is that 'allowed'? Have I not just erased that actual person entirely from my life by turning them into an unrecognizable character? Perhaps I have.

The ethical dilemmas and contradictions are many, and perhaps that is exactly why memoir, and radical memoir is such a risky, challenging, contradictory, exhilarating and exciting space to write into. We make and remake ourselves (and others) anew as we try to bring to light, the essence of our lived experience.

EXERCISE: *Life into art*

Create a scene (300 words) from the past involving friends or family members. Include dialogue, description and/or mannerisms that particularly identify them. As a reflection, consider how those people might feel about the passage on them – would they agree with your rendition of them/the situation? Why/why not?

6

Writing memoir as decolonial, genre-busting and rule-bending act

Decolonizing the self

Writing radical memoir inevitably demands that we write the so-called 'political' into the 'personal'. Our lives don't happen in isolation. Every experience is dependent on context. We grow and change impacted by the historical, cultural and political forces that shape us. Writing radical memoir asks us to understand and interrogate who we are in terms of the assumptions we make about ourselves. It would be odd if we read a memoir about Nazi Germany where the memoirist recounted his or her or their life growing up and joining the Hitler Youth without mentioning the war or interrogating their own propagandistic upbringing. Memoir is a place where the writing of a single life can become a detangling or unravelling of our political and historical selves.

Paul

My memoir *Soldier Blue* is my attempt to understand precisely how I grew up in a unique time and place where race and gender were clearly demarcated and enforced. I grew up in a pink bubble of propaganda, as we all do. We all grow up in a world constructed for us by the media, by our culture, our religion, our peer prejudices. A radical memoir asks us to step back and look at ourselves not in isolation but how we are in relation to our society.

The problem in using memory as the basis for writing the truth about our past is that our experience of growing up may be not actually as we think it was. Our parents, our government and the media may have shielded us from the realities around us, created a ready-made reality for us to live in. Maybe your childhood was not as illusory or as extremely shaped by propaganda as mine, but as I grew older I realized that what I thought was true as a child was not. In an interview in a Zimbabwean literary journal *Mazwi*, I was asked: 'What was it like growing up in Rhodesia?' I could have given my cosy answer – it was idyllic, I was loved, it was a peaceful innocent time – but I had grown up in a period of extreme civil unrest, and then civil war, and because I was more politically and historically aware than I had been as a child, I could give a better answer than I would have if I was not informed of those forces that helped determine my identity. The answer I gave was very different to the one I would have given earlier in my life. And perhaps would be different now.

> Growing up white in Rhodesia was quite simply a lie: whites lived in a bubble of propaganda. White Rhodesia was not Africa: it was England in the tropics. It ignored African cultures and history, and made African people invisible. At school I learned Latin, French, and Italian, but not a word of Shona or Ndebele. From my peers, I learned racism and sexism and arrogant myopia. I had a very privileged upbringing, and it was not until I was called up to fight in the Rhodesian army that I began to see through the façade of this 'Western Christian Civilisation' and experience the horror of war. The memoir chronicles my attempt to disentangle myself (unsuccessfully) from being 'Rhodesian' and from fighting in the war.
>
> (Mushakavanhu 2011)

I had grown up in a state of emergency, press censorship and UN sanctions which had effectively shut me off from the outside world, and my own perceptions had been constructed for me by a monolithic white colonial media. There was no social media in those days or alternative viewpoints, so I accepted a world view and a reality unquestioningly.

When it came to writing my memoir, if I was to be honest, I needed to show how I had been constructed as a 'white Rhodesian male self' in a political, colonial, social, geographical context. But to do this, I needed access to things I did not know as a child. My memories were not only unreliable but limited and sometimes trivial. I had to be outside of myself, have hindsight, research the events that were happening around me to which I was oblivious if I wanted to understand who I was.

This is not to say you have to invalidate your own memory and experience. My perception of myself and my experience of the world was genuine, but it needed contextualizing if I was to understand myself better. In *Soldier Blue* I parallel often what my (naive) memory is of my past with what was really going on around me. For example, in this extract, I have just taken Bianca to the school dance and she ducks out half way through, leaving me heartbroken. But I ground and contextualize, even juxtapose this teen drama (which could have happened anywhere in the world) with what was happening at that time in the country. The result is a deeper narrative that casts the school dance in an eerie light.

"I'm going home," said Bianca to some higher authority in the sky. "My brother is waiting for me. He caused this mess."

"No, Bianca," I called. "Wait." But she swished her evening dress – blue silk, strapless – to the entrance of the hall. I had not seen her brother yet, but had to believe he existed, if he was somehow the cause of all this trouble.

On that night, the night I walked home by myself and felt the warm wind blowing cold through me, police raided Tafara township and arrested fifteen people, the army marched into a village in Murewa and beat ten terrorist sympathisers; another army unit arrested five suspected terrorists; a group of thirty schoolchildren were recruited and forcibly marched through the night to a training camp in Zambia; a Congregational church was closed by the government for aiding and abetting terrorists; Selous Scouts infiltrated a village in Matabeleland to catch terrorists, but only succeeded in killing two children; two tribesmen who had given information to the security forces were tortured in front of their village by guerrilla leaders as an example; four landmines were laid under dirt roads by guerrillas who had carried them on their backs from Zambia; one political activist was placed under house arrest in Harari township; and three terrorists were hanged for their crimes in Salisbury Central Prison.

(Williams 2008: 98)

I did this not to set the record straight, or show what really happened, or to deny my own experience, but rather to enrich it and understand myself better and give a perspective on my life that I did not know then.

For this juxtaposition to occur, however, there needs to be an epiphany, an 'aha' moment when the bubble bursts or the paradigm shifts, and you realize something about yourself. At the time I did not. It was only years later that I looked back and saw the bigger picture of who I was and how strange it was to have a school dance in the middle of a civil war.

EXERCISE: *Bursting the bubble*

Write a 300-word paragraph detailing a domestic event that happened in your late teens. Now do some research and add another 300-word paragraph that details some of what was happening politically around you at that time, that you may have been unaware of. Use the above sample as an example.

Shelley

I grew up in a divided society and as a result from an early age I felt I had to define myself, make myself, as I tried to make sense of who I was in Apartheid South Africa. The law separated white people from brown people from yellow people from Black people. We were classed according to skin colour. Different rules applied to us about where we could go, which hospitals would treat us, which buses we could get on, which benches we could sit on, which schools we could go to, which people we could date. Even as a child I thought this made no sense. As Paul mentioned, the political was the fiercely personal, because every law affected every aspect of people's lives, especially Black and brown people's lives. Our education systems, based on student skin tone, were entirely different, primed to hegemonically capture an entire generation and educate them towards the goal that the government assigned for your group. But my experience was very different to Paul's. My family were social activists. In *Shadow Sisters* this extract shows how my family's life was impacted by Apartheid legislation.

> Leena took on the guise of domestic servant; she played at being the maid. She did everything millions of other domestic workers did in South Africa – she cooked, she did the laundry, she cleaned – but she didn't go home to a township at night. She did not wait in exhausting queues for a taxi at the end of a hard day to take her away from leafy half-acre gardens and houses with electricity and running water to the dust-bowl townships of Soweto or Alexandra, where sewage ran down pot-holed streets and thousands of shacks hunched back to back, housing whole families. Instead, she slept in my room, which was against the law. No Group Areas Act being adhered to in this house! The Act stipulated that black people could only live in white areas as domestic workers, maids and gardeners as long as they ate and slept in the servants' quarters. But we didn't have servants' quarters. In our house, Leena didn't take a tin plate of leftover white man's food to eat out the back, like millions of other domestic workers did; she ate at our table, from a normal plate, with us.
>
> (Davidow 2018: 5–6)

EXERCISE: *The political is the personal*

What political, social, economic, religious, gender-related or racial forces or expectations shaped your identity and how did you respond to these forces? Were you aware of them or did you awaken to them later? Did you accept them or resist them? Write a short scene (300 words) where you show the subtle forces of others' expectations on your life using the above as an example.

Genre-busting and rule-bending

If a memoir is to be radical, if it is the thing that liberates the writer from narrow, apolitical, self-enclosed narratives (*what* is being written about), then it must break rules. It must set itself free, or at least be able to free itself from the confines of traditionally acceptable forms. Just because memoir aims to tell a true story does not mean that it has to be linear, chronological, in prose, in past tense, or told in a certain voice or agreeing with a certain stance, position, ideology. It doesn't. Traditional narrative structures may even be a hindrance to the telling of a true story and we encourage you to break away from what some call a masculine, colonizing, acceptable discourse that silences or speaks over other ways of being and speaking.

An excellent example of this genre-busting is Helen MacDonald's hybrid memoir, *H is for Hawk* (2014), which blends memoir with, amongst other things, a shadow biography of TH White, nature writing, Wordsworth, and training hawks with Bedouins in Abu Dhabi.

In the rest of this chapter, we offer some radical exercises which we hope will inspire you to write memoir that suits and creates your unique voice and story as you seek to reveal the deeper meaning beneath the surface experience of particular events. Sometimes, in order to best convey emotional authenticity, experimenting with form is the best way to express your 'self' and to 'decolonize the mind'.

Since writing a memoir is a [re]construction of identity that offers the opportunity to push back against traditional structures and draw on other genres, could a life-story be made up of a pastiche of other narratives? Does poetry have a role here? Can the expectations of 'correct grammar' or 'chapters' be questioned? The role of story and storyteller as educator, as guide and healer is still central in many Indigenous cultures. We can draw on this. In South Africa, Australia, the Americas, storytelling is part of Indigenous knowledge transfer. It is the teaching tool, the way knowledge and understanding are conveyed from generation to generation. In Australia there are stories that remain unchanged in their essence over tens of thousands of years. Two mountains with a smaller one in front might be a story about two parents and the baby who crawled away to find water – and found it. So when you sing that song, unchanged for 40,000 years, and the song tells you about the landscape, you will always know where to find water – you will always know where you belong in that landscape. You are a protagonist in an ancient song and the backdrop is unchanging, unbroken no matter how much time passes.

This concept is only radical to those of us who have lost our own connection to the stories that shaped our forebears – to the stories of even our grandparents and great-grandparents. Submitting our DNA to various companies to find out 'who we really are' is based on a desire to know the stories of those from whom we are descended so that we might place ourselves, our desires and losses and hopes in the context of a deeper familial narrative. There are friends we have in Australia of Aboriginal descent who can trace their lineage back thousands of generations. They don't need any DNA testing. They know who they are. Their stories and knowing inspires us to see our own story as but a strand in a larger narrative. There are many ways to tell your story. Perhaps some of these exercises will become part of your memoir. Perhaps none of them will. At the very least, they provide the opportunity for you to consider your life through the lens of different genres. The 'you' of your story will emerge as a multi-faceted reflection of your life, illuminated by the way you frame each experience.

Memoir is traditionally thought of as prose narrative in the first person. But why? Can you write as the third person, or second person point of view? Can your memoir be in poetry? Can it be illustrated? Can a writer use other genres such as fantasy? You could write your memoir as a collage of various items – narrative or epic or lyric poems, report cards, notes and letters, or … as a *Haiku*.

Your life as a *Haiku*

A *Haiku* is an ancient Japanese form of poetry, usually a three-lined poem and the Anglicized version usually patterns the form in the following way: the first line has five syllables, the second seven, the third, five, and it usually makes some leap or realization (or epiphany) in the last line. Have a look at some *Haiku* and then attempt one of your own. Imagine this as a compressed memoir of your life or as an aspect of your life. Here's an example:

> I ran from my home
> And five continents later
> Call this red land mine

EXERCISE: *Your life as a* Haiku

The *Haiku* allows you to take the universe of your experience, your life, and distil it down into a simple *Haiku*. The form comes first. Follow the form strictly.

Line 1: five syllables

Line 2: seven syllables

Line 3: five syllables

Theme: nature as metaphor; life; mortality; illumination

Fairy tales

A fairy tale is usually a story that has been passed down the generations, containing folk wisdom and distilled moral advice in the form of a fantasy story, usually involving some sort of magic. It is not generally thought of as 'true' in an autobiographical sense. But a fairy tale can tell your story effectively in its compact form. Think of Hans Christian Anderson who wrote fairy tales which were deeply autobiographical and expressed his disability, his alienation from 'normal society' and his talent for seeing through lies and speaking truth to power. You are probably familiar with 'The Ugly Duckling', 'The Emperor's New Clothes' and 'The Little Mermaid' but have another look at these fairy tales as memoirs of the author. Anderson himself felt he was an ugly duckling – literally he thought himself ugly – and his talents were often unrecognized. It is worth reading his biography to see how he struggled in life, and then see how his tales are attempts to express that struggle in fairy tale form.

EXERCISE: *Your life as a fairy tale*

Five minutes: write the beginning of your life as though you were writing a fairy tale ... stop after five minutes. You might begin with – *Once upon a time there was a little boy/girl/princess/troll called ...*

Shelley's example:

Once upon a time, there lived in a faraway land full of wild, tawny animals, a girl whose hair always looked as though she'd just woken up. ...

Paul's example:

Once upon a time there was a boy called whatyagot 123, or Bloggs. He didn't know why his father called him that, but he was an only child and he felt early in life that he had a destiny beyond whatyagot 123 ...

James Joyce's example:

Joyce's fictional autobiography, or *Künstlerroman*, *A Portrait of the Artist as a Young Man* (1916), which we would argue is a form of radical memoir, begins this way:

> Once upon a time and a very good time it was there was a moocow coming down along the road and this moocow that was coming down along the road met a nicens little boy named baby tuckoo.

(Joyce 1916: 1)

Magic realism

What if the form of a memoir did not have to be realist? Could your life be written as a fantasy, a fictional autobiography? If you can use fictional techniques to construct your memoir, you can push the parameters. You could employ other genres to serve certain purposes. Bringing magical realism into realism could add angles and texture to life-writing that allows for different facets of emotional truth to be explored – and blurs the line between fact and fiction.

Magic realism is often associated with (and some say) originated in South American postcolonial narratives that rejected the rational, realist discourse of Western imperialism, and incorporated a blending of fantastic or magical elements into a realistic portrayal of the world. As opposed to fantasy literature which is clearly not meant to be a realist portrayal of events, magical realism blurs the lines between realism and fantasy and shows a world where magic is part of everyday life. Would this technique liberate truths that are impossible to write about?

What about trying this technique in writing memoir? Magical realism challenges the material and rational assumptions we often make about what constitutes 'reality'. And since much of our life is experienced unconsciously and expressed in the language of the unconscious, what about drawing on that idea in memoir-writing?

We dream every night using the language of myth, metaphor and magic without any conscious effort. Our dreams appear to be a way that we process our experiences, helping us make sense of our daily lives through fantastic and bizarre narratives. This could be an exciting way to write about certain experiences.

Here are some of the characteristics of the genre:

1   Magic realism has fantastical elements that do not occur in the world we know but are presented as if they are ordinary and normal.

2   The magic is unexplained so that it is experienced as 'normal' and an ordinary part of life.

Shelley's example:

One evening, when the sky was pink with sunset and the birds sang go-to-bed songs from the home tree that stood outside the split-pole fence, I lay on my back on the grass, looking up at the many worlds that hung over the front yard, suspended in the sky, turning this way and that with the wind on their gossamer strings that vanished into the air. I blinked, and one of the hanging worlds fell into the garden.

Paul's example (from a dream I had which I later turned into a short story):

'Your book order.' He extended his branch-like limbs towards me.

The book he presented to me – and which I must have ordered without any recollection – was innovative to say the least. It was in the shape of a large pencil with a point at one end and an eraser at the other.

What is it?

'Your book.' He zipped it open down the middle and inside were loose thin pages, like so many pencil shavings. 'Begin anywhere.'

I held the book and leafed through the shavings. They looked as if they would crumble at the slightest touch.

(Williams, Art 2020: 34)

EXERCISE: *Magic realism*

Write a 300-word paragraph/segment of your life as a magical realist piece. In this piece, magical things happen, but you describe them as if they are everyday things. So, if an angel walks down the road, you describe this as if it's ordinary. If you're writing a dream, or something that may have been a dream, describe it as if it's real. Add magical elements into your life-story without making excuses for them or relegating them to the realm of dream/fantasy/vision and see what happens.

Radical dialogue

For hundreds of years, novelists have used epistolary conventions to convey a lot of information. Letters are one way of consolidating time and events – they summarize without boring the reader – they engage without having to go into much descriptive or temporal detail. Memoirs can be constructed using similar techniques. It's clear that very few people remember exactly what was said and when and by whom – we acknowledge that in reading memoir – did she actually say that at that day and time? We allow for the fact that dialogue is an approximation. Likewise with letters, or texts. As a memoir writer, you can use dialogue to move the plot along and create character. And that dialogue can be in the form of text messages, or written messages of any kind. It does not have to follow conventional rules. Taking that into the world of e-mails and text messages can add a realist dimension to a story. Here's an example where a few texts convey what might take pages of description and exposition to communicate:

> *Why are you so late? When will you be home?*
> *At the restaurant. Hanging with everyone. Go to sleep.*
> *Is Jess there?*
> *Yeah.*
> *Don't. Come. Home.*

EXERCISE: *Text messages*

Write a section of your life as a series of text messages that reveal what's going on as well as reveals some tension between the 'characters'. (You can use a real conversation, or parts of a real conversation if it suits you.)

The heaviness of rules (and the lightness in breaking them)

If you're writing a radical memoir you are allowed to be radical. That means breaking rules. In all creative endeavours, there are all kinds of rules, assumed, expected, that guide the writing style and the writer's construction of narrative. Knowing how to use the rules, and then breaking them can lead to innovation and radical memoir writing, in particular, rule-breaking in terms of grammar and sentence construction can create unique 'voice'.

Here's a grammatically correct sentence: *I walked to the shop slowly and consequently missed the bus.* There's nothing wrong with that sentence, but it has no personal rhythm to it – there is no 'voice', no emotive impact.

Here is a series of sentence fragments that create a quick impression of a character and situation: *Sitting alone. Her chair empty in front of the fireplace. Her heart, a black hole.*

Here again is a short paragraph made up of correct sentences, followed by the same paragraph using parataxis:

Correct sentence: *In that moment I see her. And him. I know and feel that all this waiting, hoping, wishing, writing and dreaming have come to nothing.*

Parataxis: *And in that moment I see her face as she looks at him and I know and feel that all this waiting and hoping and wishing and writing and dreaming have come to nothing.*

Parataxis is a way of making sentences do more than simply conveying information. Parataxis works by placing words side by side without the need for using coordinating conjunctions in the correct manner if at all.

Novelists use parataxis, and there is not a single reason why this shouldn't work in a memoir.

Paul

Here's an example – a build-up of events from *Soldier Blue*, a collage of images thrown together in quick succession to create a multilayered effect:

> It worries me how trivial these memories are. I didn't remember anything important, like the time I was lost and then found in the servants' kaya, eating sadza with them, to the wrath of my parents. I didn't know about the riots in the townships, the breakup of the Federation which had brought us here in the first place, or the crisis when my parents almost returned home with a pension, but then bravely stuck it out. I didn't know about the fear that oozed out of the white population at the breakup of the Great British Empire, the surrender of power, the flight of whites, and the triumph of independent dancing Africans in certain countries to the north of us. I didn't know that our own country was heading for a crisis, because it refused to join those other independent countries, and tried to turn back the clock.
>
> (Williams 2008: 8)

This paragraph also has the effect of filling out the political context of my early life not by telling the reader what I remember but by telling you what I did not know.

Here are some examples of parataxis from fiction writers you may know – it is much more prevalent in novels than in non-fiction – but since we are all in the business of creating story for emotional impact, this technique serves all writers regardless of genre:

Toni Morrison's *Sula* (1973)

Twenty-two years old, weak, hot, frightened, not daring to acknowledge the fact that he didn't know who or what he was … with no past, no language, no tribe, no source, no address book, no comb, no pencil, no clock, no pocket handkerchief, no rug, no bed, no can opener, no faded postcard, no soap, no key, no tobacco pouch, no soiled underwear and nothing nothing nothing to do … he was sure of one thing only: the unchecked monstrosity of his hands … (Hale 2022: np)

Ernest Hemingway's *A Farewell to Arms* (1929)

Troops went by the house **and** down the road **and** the dust they raised powdered the leaves of the trees. The trunks of the trees too were dusty **and** the leaves fell early that year **and** we saw the troops marching along the road **and** the dust rising and leaves, stirred by the breeze, falling **and** the soldiers marching **and** afterward the road bare **and** white except for the leaves … (Didion 1998: np)

Raymond Chandler's *Farewell My Lovely* (1940)

I needed a drink, I needed a lot of life insurance, I needed a vacation, I needed a home in the country. What I had was a coat, a hat and a gun. (Ward 2014)

EXERCISE: *Parataxis and stream-of-consciousness*

Write a 300-word paragraph about your life using the examples of parataxis to create a stream-of-consciousness effect. Place the same emotional weight on each element; or build a collection of different items, ideas or experiences that have the same 'weight'.

The difference between parataxis and hypotaxis

Parataxis tends to create a stream-of-consciousness type of narrative with several independent thoughts. Hypotaxis, on the other hand, builds several dependent clauses upon one another, forming one complete thought. Here is an example from James Baldwin's memoir *Notes of a Native Son* (1955):

> When I was around nine or ten I wrote a play which was directed by a young, white schoolteacher, a woman, who then took an interest in me, and gave me books to read, and, in order to corroborate my theatrical bent, decided to take me to see what she somewhat tactlessly referred to as 'real' plays.
>
> (Nordquist 2019: np)

EXERCISE: *Hypotaxis and emotional build-up*

Write a 300-word paragraph about your life using the example above of hypotaxis – create a build-up of emotions or different ideas that stack on each other incrementally.

Parataxis and hypotaxis can be confusing: Stanley Fish explains them in this way: 'the difference [is equivalent to] walking through a museum and stopping as long as you like at each picture [parataxis] and being hurried along by a guide who wants you to see what you're looking at as a stage in a developmental arc she is eager to trace for you [hypotaxis]' (Hale 2013: n.p.).

Playing with form is a way of breaking ranks. Writers can break with colonial and Western discourses, refuse to be limited by adherence to expected narrative structures. Why not do away with capital letters, or punctuation, or spell things differently, or include graphics, or juxtapose the order of events, or write in the present tense or start at the end of your life and work backwards, or just give short episodes rather than one coherent explanation, or do anything that reflects your life more accurately than a traditional narrative pattern?

Experiments in form

We have read various memoirs that break the conventional rules of narrative form. Memoirs do not have to be linear columns of words presenting a single narrative. A memoir can have two or three or more narratives, and these narratives can run in columns down the page, and present the reader with parallel, simultaneous, sometimes contradictory stories. Narratives can intersect each other, blend together, create patterns on the page, leave gaps, form crossword puzzles with 'down' and 'across' columns and rows.

A student of ours who is working on a memoir decided to present her life-story over as a series of stories in different genres. One chapter is her memoir as a horror story, another as a romance, another as a fairy tale, and yet another as a newspaper article. By playing with genre in this way, she gives a multi-faceted account of her experience.

EXERCISE: *Playing with form and genre*

1 Write a page of your memoir by experimenting in form – either write in several columns, each column representing different aspects of yourself, or different times, moods, places in your life, or break the form even more, disrupting the linear flow of narrative across the page, using patterns and gaps to create the story.

2 Following on from your life as a fairy tale, write a page using a genre formula such as horror or crime or fantasy or romance, or a form such as a newspaper or magazine feature article on yourself.

Conclusion

This chapter is about grounding your memoir in the appropriate context and form: we will explore more genre/rule-breaking experimental ways of writing memoir in later chapters, but consider for now that the form should reflect and respect the unique content of your memoir. Writing a memoir is a [re]construction of your identity which is complex and individual to you. Experiment, break away, create anew. Write your memoir in a form that reflects your emotional journey accurately, but also situates your self-narrative in a context – political, social, geographical, historical – that reflects accurately *who* you are but also answers the questions *when* (time) and *where* (place) and *how* and *why* (what political and social forces shaped your life).

7

Memoir as erasure

In the chapter on writing character, we discussed how writing others into your memoir can 'erase' them and replace them with your constructions of them. In this chapter, we discuss how writing about yourself may do the same. Instead of preserving your memories and your past self, writing about yourself might actually replace your past history and memory with a constructed version of yourself. This is not necessarily a bad thing – writing about yourself may also reveal how your past self is a construction already and writing about it may dismantle previous ideas you have had about yourself and deepen or alter your perspective on your life.

There is nothing outside the text

Jacques Derrida is perhaps the most influential literary and linguistic theorist from the late twentieth century. His most quoted statement 'there is nothing outside the text' (Derrida 'Il n'y a pas de hors-texte' 1976: 158) might resonate at some level with those of us who write memoir: if our aim is to capture something with our words or describe some 'reality' of our lives, then our endeavour is perhaps in vain. Words, Derrida is saying, do not describe 'reality', but shape it, create it. Anyone who has tried to write memoir or capture a 'true' event in words will know this – the minute we begin writing, we are reconstructing, approximating, creative 'avatars' not real people.

Derrida claims that we can only understand our experience of the world through language. Words are 'signifiers' that point to 'absence' but can never be reality. Memoir is not a direct copy of reality in words but a weaving of meaning using words as a net to capture some understanding of how we are written by words, weaved by language. This presents memoir writers with a radical perspective on our work and asks us to question fundamental concepts we have hitherto taken for granted.

Deconstruction

Derrida suggests that the person we call a 'self' is a 'text', a 'field', a linguistic construct. Deconstruction is Derrida's method of analysing how 'texts' have been constructed or woven. 'Text' comes from the Latin *texere* which means 'to weave'. A text is a woven web or tapestry. So if we are aware that what we think is reality is actually just a woven text, and that what we think of as our 'self' is a constructed text, then writing memoir can uncover hidden structures, demystify ideas we hold about ourselves, dissect myths about ourselves and untangle webs of meaning that we have woven around ourselves.

In previous chapters we have hinted at ways of destabilizing how we think about memoir – recording the past realistically, capturing our memories in words, portraying our friends and family as characters. But the fundamental problem with this 'normal' view, as we have seen, is that writing memoir is not a simple act of recording what happened; it is essentially an understanding of how we have been constructed, how we construct ourselves in language, and then re-create that 'self' in words, using language. And this is a very different thing to describing 'what really happened'. It is wise to acknowledge this provisionality. In the following pages we will demonstrate how we have down this in our own memoirs, beginning with a case study of *Soldier Blue*.

Paul

My memoir *Soldier Blue* took me twenty years to write and is a process of what Derrida would call 'deconstruction' and 'writing under erasure'. But I did not start with theory and plan to write a Derridean deconstruction of my life.

I wrote as best as I could to understand it as I went along and only afterwards realized that I was deconstructing, not constructing.

I was motivated by a number of things. First was a desire to understand who I was. What was the meaning of all I had experienced in the war, and how had it made me what I was today? Secondly, I wanted to tell others my story, to explain to others what I was doing in Africa, what was it like in the war. Thirdly, and related to this last reason, I wanted to preserve history, to get the story straight for myself as I was starting to forget or retell the story and reframe it, and myths about the war were starting to harden into fact. Wild claims were being made which I knew were not correct. Fourthly, I wanted to heal something in my past, deal with my PTSD and use the writing to do it. Fifthly, and perhaps the most importantly, I had the urge, the ache to write the story to express myself, to create art out of my life.

Realist phase

During my military service in the Rhodesian war, I began to write down events that happened to me, because they were so unbelievable and shocking that I knew no one would believe me, and that I might begin to doubt what I had been through. I wanted a record of the atrocities and absurdities of war. After the war, I wrote up the journal, called it *Rhodesians Never Die* (a bitterly ironic reference to a patriotic song), attempting to answer Doris Lessing's call that writing memoir was the counter to state propaganda:

> The people who fought in that war and know what it was like are in their twenties and thirties. Soon at least some will be writing their memories, autobiographies, reminiscences. Then the truth about the War will be exposed, and there will be two versions, the official histories and the truth – Doris Lessing, *African Laughter*.
>
> (Williams 2008: iv)

When I first began writing *Soldier Blue*, I believed that what I was doing was telling the truth, as honestly as I could, about my experiences growing up as a young white man in Rhodesia (now Zimbabwe). I was, as Lejeune had pointed out, author and narrator and protagonist. What could be simpler?

As for narrative technique, honesty was my method, if honesty can be called a method. In the attempt to get to the 'real truth' about my life, I had to recall, as honestly as possible, my experience of growing up in this British colony from 1960 to 1980. And being honest entailed the possibility that I was wrong, that my perception might not actually be the truth.

> I was a racist. The word did not exist then, not in Rhodesia; but my world view had been constructed on the premise that whites were right, Britannia ruled the waves, that Rhodesia saves and Zimbabwe ruins. My world was black and white. All that was good came from white civilisation. All that was bad came from Africanisation. I was a self-righteous teenager, and to me my ideas were obviously, self-evidently true. All my friends and neighbours, the government, all Rhodesians knew that we were doing the right thing, that this was how things were. Even black people knew which side their bread was buttered on. All except my dense parents.
>
> (Williams 2008: 73)

On the book's publication, honesty as a theme was highlighted by both readers and critics.

> A vivid story of coming of age in a country falling apart, told with wry, dry, self-deprecating honesty.
>
> A lucid, insightful and unflinchingly honest account of what it was like growing up during the last days of white rule.
>
> The uncompromising honesty of the author, and the page-turning power of the story, will reward almost any reader.
>
> His book is also more than just the usual nostalgic trawl down memory lane. For one thing he is too honest.
>
> 'Makes you glad he [Author] was around to keep tabs on events.
>
> 'Soldier Blue' is more honest than *Mukiwa* ...'
>
> (Williams 2013: np)

Modernist phase

But was I being honest? Was I being accurate and objective? Many of the people portrayed in my memoir would disagree with how I portrayed them; my interpretation of history was mine. Even if I tried to be objective, memory was faulty. Selective. Wrong, according to my present self.

I realized that I was not able to write a 'true' memoir, but only true to myself and how I perceived it. My modern self was not patriotic, did not glorify war, did not demonize the enemy as so many memoirs about this war did. So I rewrote the memoir, acknowledging my bias, and called it *The Green and White*.

I could do this by adding another perspective. My younger self was very different to the person I am today. If I was writing about that past self from the perspective of my present self, those two selves were not the same person. There was a discrepancy, but also an awareness that I was constructing that past self out of a set of faulty memories and perceptions, and gaps. So I added an older wiser narrator to give perspective. I also added other voices, contradictory voices, so that we would have a kaleidoscope of perspectives, as Faulkner did in *As I Lay Dying* and *Sound and the Fury*, both modernist novels.

Before the whites came, he said, it was paradise. No one owned anything; we were one. We were the blue dome of sky, the chinkling pebbly rivers of Nyanga, the scraggly Msasa trees clutching whispered spells from the wind, the roar of mosi-oa-tunya. We lived in peace and serenity. Then one day people without knees arrived and squatted on our land. At first they did not bother us, merely scrabbled for shiny stones in the ground. …

What a load of codswallop, said Kloppers. Before the whites came, Africa was a dark continent of disease and intertribal war. The whites rescued the Shona from being slaves of the Matabele. When we arrived, the land was vacant, with the huddled Shona living in fear in stony forts in Inyanga, eating millet and at the superstitious mercy of an inhospitable universe full of wild animals, monsters and cruel gods. We saved the ungrateful Calibans from their own nightmares. We brought roads, the railway, schools, medicine and democracy.

(Williams 2008: 17)

Underlying the fragmented narrative, however, was a solid truth, the 'real' truth. A complexity of contradictory narratives still pointed to what 'really' happened, but it was a more complex reality, one that incorporated a theoretical lens, political context and historical perspective that there were two sides to every story. To get to the truth you needed both sides. I also explored a mythical thread in my life that I had not noticed before. I was reading Robert Graves and Jung at the time and realized that my younger self was pursuing some archetypal quest for the 'white goddess' an ancient cult-ritual that disrupted the monotheistic patriarchal religions and this helped me make sense of my younger self's biography.

Post-modernist phase

Still I felt this was not an accurate memoir of myself. It was too neat, too ordered and shaped into a crisis and resolution, and life was not like that. Life for me was more an unanswered series of questions. I left the memoir for years, and only when I was living in Florida in the early 2000s I began to find the way to write it. And that was 'aslant' (see the later chapter where Roland Barthes discusses this writing method). I had just read *Slaughterhouse 5* which is (I would argue) Kurt Vonnegut's disguised war memoir where he uses humour, experimental narrative devices and fragmentary narratives in order to write about his traumatic experiences in the Second World War. He had also spent years trying to find the right way to write his experience, to look back on his younger self and make sense of what had happened. 'That was I. That was me. That was the author of this book,' he admits (Vonnegut 1972: 59), and the reader realizes that he is not even the main protagonist in his own story. And that the only sense he can make of the war experience is by using fictional version of himself, and finally just a bird call – 'Poo-tee-weet' (Vonnegut 1972: 97).

In 2006 I found the voice and style needed to get the critical distance from my younger self to be able to write about him. It had taken me twenty years to be able to understand what I was doing and how to say it. Not that you should have to take that long! I took the long road – you use the shortcuts.

I realized that what I had been doing was using various frames of narratives to try to make sense of my life. I decided to look at how I was writing the self. As Salman Rushdie puts it, instead of using the mirror to reflect reality (realism) or writing about how the mirror reflects reality (modernism), I was 'writing about the mirror' (Rushdie 1979) as a device to create the illusion of a 'reality' (postmodernism). I was also aware that I could not simply write a white man's story, a colonial tale where such writers have 'used Africa as a kind of backdrop where white characters were permitted to work out their neuroses in rather stock patterns' (Larson 1972: 278), but a postcolonial narrative, aware of politics, race and the 'construction' of a self in that context. I had woven a text.

I have often used the following analogy to differentiate between Realism, Modernism and Postmodernism, using literary texts. This passage comes from my book *Novel Ideas: Writing Innovative Fiction* (Williams 2020: 112–13).

Alfred Tennyson's poem, 'The Lady of Shallott' (1833), describes the Realist relation of art to reality. The artist, a woman constructing a tapestry, copies reality outside and recreates it in her tapestry. The medium used to relay the information is a mirror which sharply divides the two realms of reality and art so when the woman turns to look directly at reality she breaks the sharp line of the distinction and hence her artwork is destroyed.

A postmodernist correction of this view of art and reality is given by Thomas Pynchon in *The Crying of Lot 49* (1965) where Oedipa Maas describes a painting of a number of girls in a tower,

> Embroidering a kind of tapestry which spilled out of the slit windows and into a void, seeking hopelessly to fill the void: for all the other buildings and creatures, all the waves, ships and forests of the earth were contained in this tapestry, and the tapestry was the world.
>
> (Pynchon 1966: 11–12)

Pynchon's view of art is that reality is a void and art is a construction that fills the void. Rather than serving as a reflection of reality, art becomes itself, the reality that exists: 'Fiction cannot be a representation of reality, or an imitation, or even a recreation of reality, it can only be a reality' (Federman 2011: 147).

If you look back at the photo you wrote about in Chapter 1, you were writing about the 'reality' reflected in the photo. But if you write about the photo itself, how it creates (false and nostalgic) meaning, how the memory is constructed, then you are deconstructing this image, reading it and your past self as a 'text' created through language.

If you were to write about that photo in the light of Derrida's notion of 'nothing outside the text', perhaps you would talk about *differance*, what is not in the photo, what binaries are privileged what is erased. Immediately I would see in my photo a bunch of wealthy, privileged white people, happy, healthy, confident (except me!). Was I the odd one out here, the outsider, unable to fit this utopian frame? What is erased here is that this is colonial Rhodesia in the middle of a war and the white population is small minority in power. Secondly the girls are relatively modestly dressed according to the cultural norms of the era. They are segregated, girls on left, boys on right. It is okay for boys to be scantily dressed but not the girls. The binarized sexes seem comfortable with each other. And with themselves as male/female. But I was often called 'girly' because my behaviour and appearance often disturbed those binaries. Thirdly if I was to 'write about the mirror', the photo is faded and unfocused. Unlike digital technology this is light on paper, a different capturing of imagery. Slightly off centre, a long shot that seems to reveal that the photographer is not aiming correctly. I could go on ...

The major problem I faced in rewriting my memoir (which ultimately became *Soldier Blue*) was that I now knew I was no longer recounting truth, or reality, but imposing a modern-day frame over it, and that my initial research method (dredging up memories and recording them down as accurately as possible) did not produce an accurate picture of who I was. My memories were unreliable, constructed and sometimes trivial. There was a war going on, and I was unaware of it. The British Empire was breaking up, and I had no idea. So how could I write a memoir when I knew I did not know about the past and that my self was text, already written by my culture? The only way I could do this honestly was to write about the unreliability of my memories and how I was constructed, using erasure to reveal what was underneath this written self/text.

> They [my parents] arrived in Rhodesia, *the story goes*, with a pram full of saucepans, a few shillings jangling in their pockets, and an optimistic trust in a benevolent universe, that things would somehow work out. *That's how they tell it, anyhow.*
>
> (Williams 2008: 2 italics mine)

It is unsettling because the story may be true, but I am erasing it with those words in italics, and this act of erasure undermines its claim for truth. It sounds rather likes a 'story', a fiction, which of course, like all historical accounts, it is.

In order to expose the 'gaps' and contradictions in the narrative, I brought in another fictive prop – the frame-narrator: not just the older, wiser 'Paul' who could 'tell the truth' about what was 'really' going on, who could see the chinks in this monolithic colonial discourse, but one who actually undermined the credibility of the narrative itself, who created an ironic discrepancy between the past and present self. He speaks in the italics.

> My first memory *apparently* is a stark image of the white bars of my cot, a square, mauve wallpapered room. … *I am also told that* I waved goodbye to my mother every morning as she guiltily drove off to work … But I really only remember from about the age of four onward, and I only remember insignificant fragments of my life in media res. … *It worries me how trivial these memories are. I didn't remember anything important, like the time I was lost and then found in the servants' kaya, eating sadza with them, to the wrath of my parents. I didn't know about the riots in the townships, the breakup of the Federation which had brought us here in the first place, or the crisis when my parents almost returned home with a pension, but then bravely stuck it out. I didn't know about the fear that oozed out of the white population at the breakup of the Great British Empire, the surrender of power, the flight of whites, and the triumph of independent dancing Africans in certain countries to the north of us.*
>
> (Williams 2008: 7, 8 italics mine)

My past self is being constructed here out of unreliable and seemingly insignificant memories. I was weaving a text. This is when I changed the title of the book to *Soldier Blue*, a reference to a propaganda song I listened to at the time that helped in my identity formation of what a 'soldier' was and how my 'self' had been constructed from broken images. *Soldier Blue* is also an American film about war, making my memoir a palimpsest. *Soldier Blue* is also named after one of my most traumatic experiences in the war, watching a soldier die by being crushed under a truck and turning blue.

Memoir as fiction

Writing *Soldier Blue* made me realize that in order to keep readers engaged, and as we have repeatedly advised in this book, I needed to use narrative strategies and techniques that are usually used in writing fiction. For both memoir and fiction, you need a compelling beginning or 'hook' that draws readers in, you need foreshadowing to keep them reading, you need cliff hangers, crises, plot points, memorable characters, sensory setting, a compelling style. In other words, to write good memoir, you need to become a good fiction writer and develop storytelling and literary skills so that your memoir will be read. I thought of my memoir as a novel, with its protagonists and antagonists, its major and minor characters, its plot points, vivid setting and having an authentic voice.

Point of view

I decided that – like most memoirs – mine would be told from first-person point of view, as is typical of memoir. Lejeune maintains that the author and narrator and character must be the same, must be the 'I' of the story for it to hold to the reader-writer contract. Yes, in *Soldier Blue*, they are all the same person (me), but the 'I' who is telling the story is an older, wiser 'I' to the 'I' who is being told. The 'I' who is the child and teenager is an unreliable narrator – the naive younger version of me who did not know as much as the reader does, as I have described above. This is not unusual – a memoir is typically told from the point of view of a wiser, older author who looks back and tells us the story of their life, but I decided that an unreliable narrator was more accurately how I was as I grew up so I added a frame narrator, a present-day older and more omniscient narrator who could comment on and fill the gaps the younger narrator did not know about. I took my cue from a number of novels that use this device effectively, and though they are not memoirs, the authors use the genre or frame of the confessional memoir to tell their story. My primary exemplars here were Charles Dickens's *David Copperfield* (1849), Mark Twain's *The Adventures of Huckleberry Finn* (1884) and J. D. Salinger's *Catcher in the Rye* (1951). In the latter two, the first-person unreliable narrator directly addresses the reader, and the reader soon realizes that the narrator does not know as much as the reader and sometimes gets it wrong.

Hybridized characters

I had way too many characters, as I was writing about my whole childhood and teenage hood up to where I left the army and went to university, and I had interacted with hundreds of people, and had dozens of close friends (and enemies!), so I had to select only a few and decide who I could include in the memoir. I had to change the names of people so they would not be offended or inclined to sue me; I created composite characters made up of many people; I invented conversations, dialogues and exchanges that could not possibly be historically accurate or remembered in their entirety. The female 'love interest' and person I was in love with in the story, Bianca Pennefather, was a fiction, a composite figure of all the girls I had fallen in love with and gone out with in those teenage years. The school and army bully, Craig Hardy, likewise was a hybrid of many of the bullies I had to deal with in school and in my military training. In this way I could get to the essence of the experience of my romantic and bullying experience and be true to that experience.

Plot, beginnings, plot spoilers, *in medias res* and hooks

I wanted the narrative to follow a Freytag's pyramid plot structure with its initial conflict, crisis, climax, denouement and resolution; I had to be selective in my material in order to shape the essential story and compress many events into one. And I decided to begin with a whole summary of the events that take place, which is somewhat of a plot spoiler, I admit, but one I felt necessary so I could forewarn my readers that this was going to be a tragedy and to foreshadow the events to give them more pathos. Writing about the early idyllic years of my childhood needed the dark shadow of impending doom hanging over it if I wanted readers to turn the pages.

> When my parents decided to go to Africa in September 1958, they didn't know they were stumbling into the beginnings of a civil war that would spiral into political madness, and end in economic ruin and poverty. They didn't know that their only son would be coerced into fighting in the war. Nor did they know that in the early hours of the new millennium, they would have to flee the Dark Continent, leaving their house, car, servant, bank account, and forty-six-year old suntan.
>
> (Williams 2008: 5)

However, when I sent off the memoir to publishers, they did not like this beginning. They suggested it should begin like a best-selling novel. Did I have an event I could put in at the beginning that was gripping, unputdownable to hook the reader, instead of the usual 'I was born …'? I lifted a passage from the end of the novel, a plane crash I was meant to be in.

3 SEPTEMBER 1978

The Air Rhodesia Vickers Viscount 'Hunyani' banked to the left and bumped lightly through the cumulonimbus cloudbank on its ascent from Kariba. In five minutes, flight RH 825 was already out of sight of the control tower, speeding into the haze of a September African evening. The only evidence of its passage was a brown smear across a tawny sky. The cicadas began singing in the grass lining the runway, and the airport prepared to close for the night. …

A bang shook the aircraft. It lurched to one side, plunged into a giant air pocket and spun ninety degrees, east to south. The two newly-weds clutched each other and stared out of the starboard window. Flames and smoke poured from the first engine. A metal fragment thunked past. The plane shuddered again, and the second engine burst into flames. Black smoke rushed past the window; intense heat radiated through the thick glass into the cabin. One man drew the blinds. "Put your head between your knees and hold your ankles," another told his wife. The No Smoking and Fasten Seat Belt signs blinked on, and the two air hostesses rushed to the front of the plane.

(Williams 2008: 1)

Soldier Blue now began *in medias res* and then took reader back to the 'I was born …' beginning which gave the narrative an ominous foreshadowing and foreboding, and readers had read all the way to the end of the book to find out what happened in the plane crash and why I had so closely missed dying in it.

EXERCISE: *Beginnings*

Write a 300-word beginning of your memoir – begin at a tense or action-paced moment, *in medias res,* an exciting episode you take from later in the memoir – the most exciting or tense part of your story. Do not give us the whole scene, just a teaser, a taste, a foreshadowing of what is to come. Read this to someone and ask if they would read on …

Settings, style, voice

Settings were compounded into one or two central locations; three places became one; ten trips to the frontline of the war became three; I borrowed rhetorical devices from Vladimir Nabokov, J. M. Coetzee, Martin Luther King, from Zulu praise-poetry to create a style and voice that was reflective of the time.

To assure my readers that I was not breaking the reader/writer contract, I wrote the disclaimer you have seen in a previous chapter to claim that I was still accountable to 'truth' ('truth' of course in any postmodern or poststructural discourse needs parentheses).

All these narrative techniques used in fiction – and more – should be used in memoir too to get readers to want to read on. It is a fine balance. You need to keep the reader/writer contract, tell your true story as honestly as you can, but it needs to be constructed and shaped so that it is compelling and gets to the heart of who you are.

Emotional truth

How memoir writers have justified using fiction in their so-called truthful memoirs is by claiming 'emotional truth'. Sacrifice too much 'fact' for narrative unity and you cross the Scholes spectrum line into fiction. But the measure of a memoir's effectiveness is not what literally happened, which in some cases we may not remember or will never know, but 'emotional truth':

> We each have our own emotional truth. That truth might not be exactly factually correct, but what is important for the person writing memoir is how they recall the event and what meaning they make out of it for their lives. I don't mean, in any way, that they fabricate the event. What I mean is that they take an actual event and replicate it to the best of their recollection.
>
> (Murdock 1982: 1)

> Perhaps it never did snow that August in Vermont; perhaps there never were flurries in the night wind, and maybe no one else felt the ground hardening and summer already dead even as we pretended to bask in it, but that was how it felt to me, and it might as well have snowed, could have snowed, did snow.
>
> (Didion 1969: 2)

'What happened to the writer is not what matters; what matters is the larger sense that the writer is able to make of what happened' (Gornick 1996: 5).

Ken Kesey's narrator of *One Flew over the Cuckoo's Nest* (1962) suggests: 'It's the truth, even if it didn't happen' (Kesey 1962: 1).

This looks to be a contradiction. Memoir is about being accountable to the 'facts', to what 'really happened', but as we have argued, the idea of an objectively retrievable, verifiable past is an illusion. Accountability to historical fact is a fallacy as 'fact' is a construction. The rhetorical device of confessional honesty is an illusion.

EXERCISE: *Emotional truth*

Write a 300-word scene from your past that was intensely memorable and describe it as you feel it was, not necessarily as it happened. Create dialogue that may not be exact but that conveys the spirit of what was said.

Soldier Blue is not then a memoir about what happened, but about how my 'truth' was constructed, about how I had to disentangle myself from what I thought was the truth. My memoir was a deconstruction of how memoir is written, a radical memoir that questions how narrative is constructed.

EXERCISE: *Two selves*

Using the above example, write a 300-word paragraph about an incident where you returned to a place from the past – your old country, house, school. Describe the experience of the current reality, superimposing it on how you experienced it in the past, and how it looked back then. Map the emotional distance between then and now.

Self-erasure

The Derridean idea of self-erasure seems to go against the very notion of what memoir is, which is to make yourself visible, to create a space for yourself in words. 'Here I am! I was here!'

But sometimes writing about yourself is more about dismantling the false narratives surrounding you, the dismantling of the language systems used to create your identity for you and the contextualizing of your true self from what you once believed, or what others said you were.

> It is hard to believe that these roads, small and tattered, once ran with dreams of pursued white goddesses, and that the self I am attempting to retrieve from here is a petty, insignificant one who played no role in history, except to be one of the many whites trapped in a box, thinking they were at the centre of the world.
>
> There are thirteen million people in Zimbabwe at this time, nearly three times the population of 1971. The whites constitute an irrelevant 0.1 per cent. Even in 1971, with the white population at 2.5 per cent, we were a tiny minority. How did we presume such significance?
>
> (Williams 2008: 396)

Conclusion

Writing memoir to try to record the past is naïve, impossible, delusory. We replace the past memories with written ones, restructure our past according to our present. But that does not mean we are not recapturing something of our past selves. We need to be honest, to the point of being able to acknowledge that the reader/writer contract is not that easy to fulfil. Memoir cannot tell us the truth; it is not a mirror, but it is a record of how we see ourselves. It is a journey into the emotional truths of our lives, an emotional journey into the deep wounds of our lives, where we go to exorcize our demons, to pick out the splinters that have gone septic, the wounds that have festered. A memoir is in some ways a secular confession to the world so that we can be cleansed and healed.

8

Collective memoir

Shelley

I don't know if there exists yet a recognized, defined literary genre called 'Collective Memoir'. I want to therefore propose that it can exist, and does exist, and that it is both unique and radical. I also want to define it as something that deviates and even pushes hard against the already established academic definitions of 'collective memoir' and 'collective biography' because what I call 'collective memoir' is entirely focused on the value of creativity and story-making between people, and does not see the creative work generated as 'data' to be 'harvested', nor does it place any emphasis on the academic or didactic educational 'value' of the work, or on building or subscribing to a theoretical framework.

So, here's my definition of 'Collective Memoir' as a literary genre: it is *the process and product of a craft-focused creative writing journey by more than one writer in order to generate a memoir with more than one voice as a work of literary merit.*

There is, of course, academic writing which already defines collective memoir – but according to specific academic outcomes. In particular I'd like to refer to a thesis entitled *Collective memoir as public pedagogy: a study of narrative, writing, and memory.* Here, Elizabeth Claire-Robson poses the following research question, among others: 'How can these writing processes be theorized and understood as educational events? … Writing processes are then seen as data mines which can be analysed to generate understanding of them as 'educational events' (Clare-Robson 2011). This defines the process of a group of women reading and writing together for an academic (theoretical and educational) outcome. The 'collective memoir' puts its focus on theorizing reading and writing experience for a didactic purpose. This is rather like doing a painting for the purpose of theorizing the process and then writing about that process rather than learning how to paint for the purpose of producing a piece of art that in and of itself moves and inspires viewers to have a unique and undirected response.

Likewise, the methodology, that is, 'collective biography', has offered academics the opportunity to focus on the value of writing together, but for the purpose of analysis – that is, turning the psycho-emotional experience of, for example, women writing together into research and effectively mining that experience for data that can then be theorized and published in respectable journals. It's best defined, I believe, as follows: 'Collective biography is a qualitative, feminist methodology that uses the researchers' own written memories about a set of experiences as texts for collective analysis' (Hawkins, Falconer Al-Hindi, Moss & Kern 2016).

I've done this myself and it's not without value – for example, in my recent article *Walking towards a valuable academic life* (Manathunga, Black & Davidow 2020), two colleagues and I, exhausted by the demands of academia to publish or perish in peer-reviewed journals (and tempted to choose 'perish' on a daily basis), came up with an idea that supported us: what if we went on beach walks together to rejuvenate our tired souls? And further, what if then our walking and reflecting together could be turned into writing, and what if our collective reflections on our experiences on walking across the land (Australia), understanding our position as walkers across ground steeped in silenced Indigenous history and a multitude of stories that had gone before, could be valuable as research? What if? And so, we did it – it was a lovely experience – no question. We walked together every Friday, wrote poetry and then put it all together, framed it within respectable theory, and got published in a high-quality academic journal. Our focus was on generating material that we could then theorize and package into a specific paradigm – not on creating art – or an artefact that would have literary or artistic merit. We were generating data. Though our creative pieces could potentially have literary merit if we focused on crafting them for that purpose. A comment by one of the peer-reviewers made me laugh. The person wrote something like, *why don't the authors just go for a walk and enjoy walking?* – yeah, exactly. Collective biographies and stories shared by several attempt to highlight the validity of a multiplicity of voices telling them the same story. They do offer an opportunity for a single narrative to have multiple contributors – but they're not trying to create *art*.

Paul

Memoir is by its very definition an individual, personal account of one's life. Or is it? There is no reason why it should be. The idea of an individual, autonomous self is itself a fiction. The question 'Who are you?' may be answered in different ways, and for some it is interconnectedness that defines a self, not a fully autonomous, free Kantian self existing in isolation. And likewise a memoir could be a collective story of a community, a family, a friendship, or any combination of 'selves'. A memoir could be a conversation between two or more people with intertwining lives. There are examples of collective novels, even though the novel is assumed to be the work of one individual, such as two university colleagues of mine have done, writing to each other in a dialogue that revealed their respective histories. A collective memoir could do the same, offer an intersubjectivity of perspectives. The closest I could find to this was Alexis Wright's *Tracker* (2015), a collaborative story about visionary Aboriginal leader Bruce 'Tracker' Tilmouth, comprising interviews of more than fifty people (family, friends, politicians, even Tracker himself) to form chronological mini memoirs. But I would argue that this is more biography.

Writing the Radical Memoir is a collective memoir of sorts too, as both Shelley and I reveal our respective histories in this book and interweave our stories.

EXERCISE: *Other voices – alone or with others*

Write three or more paragraphs that define a particular event in your life. It could be an accident, a wedding, a pivotal moment. Use a different voice for each of these paragraphs. You might use your mother telling the story, a eulogy, a report. Then a newspaper clipping (real or created) or your own diary entry. If you have a partner to write with, a sibling, a close friend, give them the task of writing one of those paragraphs to juxtapose with yours. Be fearless about the result – expect or anticipate contradiction – and focus on the process of making this mosaic.

Memoir is most often thought of as a singular story and the opportunity to stand as closely in one person's shoes as is possible without being that individual. The expectation is that a memoir promises a reader unique and individual experience of the world that approximates truth or more accurately honesty and authenticity, drawing that reader out of their own perspective and into the perspective of another. But there is no reason why this experience cannot be plural.

Shelley

The idea of a collective memoir, a harmony and counterpoint expression of experience is rare. I will mention again, *Mothertongue* (2022), *Three Women* (2019) and also *Not Just Black and White* (2015) written by a mother and a daughter – Lesley and Tammy Williams – who both talk to the reader as though the reader were an interviewer, as they tell their story of trying to find out what happened to Lesley's wages that had been kept when she lived and worked as a domestic servant in Cherbourg Aboriginal Settlement in Queensland, Australia. The focus is on a single journey and quest – to find out what happened to the money. The relationship between the two authors – mother and daughter – is not at the centre of the narrative. They tell the same story from two points of view – one picking up where the other leaves off. The story is autobiographical in tone and content – the focus is not so much on the art, as on the recording of an experience – yet still it serves as a dual narrative, illuminating two perspectives on a single storyline.

It is into the radical space of plural memoir that friend Shaimaa Khalil and I wrote *Runaways* (2022).

Shaimaa and I did not set out to be innovative and daring. We had always had a close bond through letters to one another. She is a journalist, I'm a writer, but we met when we were student and teacher in Qatar in the Middle East. I was the teacher, from South Africa. She was the student, from North Africa. I am Jewish, she is Muslim. Both strangers to the desert of Qatar, we formed an almost immediate bond.

Our friendship has lasted for more than twenty years, across continents. We are so different and yet at a soul-level – so alike.

When Shaimaa was posted as the Australia correspondent in Sydney in 2019, we were so excited to finally be on the same continent. We thought we'd get to see each other every month at least, hang out, maybe write something together.

But then Covid hit, and we were locked down, locked out from each other. We began to write to each other – pieces that we called 'blobs' remembering the three years we spent together in Doha, Qatar, she as a young student, and me as a young teacher.

In writing *Runaways,* the process of constructing inexperience from two points of view had an impact that was both liberating and transformative in terms of what the genre of memoir could do. One story elicited the next. In this book Shaimaa and I wrote incrementally, to keep connected through memory. We were also trying to evoke the sensory and emotional experience of what it was like then – and how that made us who we are today. I was her teacher and entering a world that was as foreign to me as another planet. The most important element for me as a writer here was the process of creating a story without any preconceived idea of what we were doing or what it might look like. We did not know at all when we set out what shape or form this book would take. The process-as-product is something that I believe in enough to risk letting the book evolve spontaneosly. I say risk, because it does not aim to be something flashy – and as such, the value may lie only in the doing of it, and not what it becomes. But that was the point. We didn't want to take energy away from the process, and we did not focus on the book as a product until it was almost done, and yet we were aware that we were part of a making. We were creating an artefact. In a sense we were writing into the spaces created by the French feminists: there was no linear expectation and the narrative cycled in on itself although I had a sense of an underlying narrative arc. We allowed for our writing and stories to evolve as tributaries into other territories that even meandered, digressed from the 'plot'. We wrote in our individual voices *to* each other. One of the most transformative experiences was the fact that I knew that my words were going to be read with the gentleness and care that gave me permission to be most fully myself. There's something about being held in the heart of your reader that allows for a different kind of writing. That's what we did for each other. So, though we were talking to an audience, we were also talking to each other.

In the first draft our agent said that sometimes it felt that when we refer to each other too much, the reader was shut out, and so it was important to have that perspective as we went through our next draft and took out some of the times we addressed each other so that the reader was part of the worlds that we were trying to share. There are many levels that a collective memoir such as this allows writers to explore. There is always of course each individual story. But then there is another story that develops in the white spaces, and in the silences between the two stories. There are also many things left unsaid that we hint at. There are threads that we left hanging, and because this is not an autobiography that is written at the end of someone's life, we knew as we wrote that we risked an unsatisfactory ending. And yet when the process was done we knew that it was done. We were surprised. As though we came to the top of the mountain and suddenly realized we were there. For both of us the writing process was a healing journey in which we were able to take fragmented bits of our lives and put them together much like a puzzle. The wider level that this touched was that our backgrounds are historically oppositional. Muslims and Jews are not supposed to be friends. We have a deep and abiding and unlikely connection that allows us to look honestly at issues that one person alone could not easily tackle. We hold each other's stories and in doing so keep the readers in the space of tension. Shaimaa grew up in Alexandria in Egypt as a young Muslim girl shaped by a society and expectations that she had to push against constantly. I grew up in Johannesburg and Cape Town in South Africa shaped by the Apartheid regime. There was gross political injustice. Human rights did not exist for the majority of South Africans. I railed against being part of this divided society where every moment of existence was defined by race, skin colour, background.

Being able to write about these things to someone who grew up in a different culture – being able to be seen and heard by my fellow writer – was a valuable experience.

The process then of writing this collective memoir in which our two voices and styles interwove was unique. It pulled us together. It was a process of self-definition. It was different to writing a memoir with a single voice and throwing your words into the space where there is no immediate feedback. We gave feedback to each other all the time. We were in dialogue. We gave each other oxygen.

But then we had to cut and delete.

The full manuscript was as raw and open as we were, as true to our lives as we could make it but we had to decide to leave out chunks of the narrative, to protect identities.

As a single author, navigating this territory is tricky. But in a collective, deleting a thread in one person's story impacts the response from the other person. Constructing the collective memoir means that there is the potential for a collective unravelling of the narrative too.

This is something I do alone and now with others. Before submitting any memoir to a publisher, do a risk/benefit analysis: what do you want to keep in, what do you leave out? At which point are you feeling censored? At which point are you willing to risk impacting a relationship for the sake of your 'truth'?

In the end, I can say – we weighed our words, our stories, against the lives and loves who featured in our collective story. We left things out, rewrote things. We stitched around silences sometimes to show the shape of a void – understanding that sometimes it's in the white spaces that the most powerful elements of the narrative reside. A true story is not made up of a single strand. A narrative is always a tapestry made up of thousands of strands – different colours, different patterns – and when you're writing with someone else, you are working to create a whole picture not just focused on your part – and this requires you as a co-writer to ebb and flow, to find out how you serve your art, the collective voice, without sacrificing too much.

Writing a memoir of any kind is humbling.

Writing a collective memoir is a radical undoing of self as well as a re-creation of selves and it is not for everyone. *Three Women* is one example. *Mothertongues* is another. The risk of writing something messy is higher when more than one author is involved in telling a true story. But the danger of a narrow view of events is mitigated. Take your pick.

If my voice were stopped for any reason I would feel like my existence would be under threat. And yet there are times when I've had to hold back, delete or take out whole sections, because the real impact on real people in the world had to be considered.

By the time we finished writing *Runaways* we had taken ourselves apart, thread by thread, pulled the story open and then written it back together again. Life was the material for our art, but our art impacted our lives, our relationships, our discussions.

The radical memoir does not exist in a void. It is shaped out of the messy, potent cauldron of the everydayness of our existence. It is about real experiences (ours) but it drags in the people in our lives, and their real experiences, and writers need to know what this means.

Runaways created us anew, both individually and together as friends. The book was a radical journey into the art of making a book out of the raw lived back-and-forth of a long-term friendship. It included poetry, a chronological account of our time together in Qatar, and other people's stories. It included silence and spaces where we left things out or took things out. Sometimes what we left out was what we felt most connected to. What's left in the silence afterwards is an essential part of the story. We allowed for our own divergent thoughts, and we aimed for convergence, not compliance. The result is a tapestry, and any flaws have become an integral part of its organic design. Read the instructions in the exercise below. Then have a look at the extract – two small sections from the beginning of *Runaways*, where Shaimaa and I write our own stories, looping each other in. The memoir is not a series of letters to one another, and it includes the reader – only sometimes alerting the reader to the fact that we are talking to each other, sharing, along the way.

EXERCISE: *The power of two voices* (see the example from *Runaways* which follows)

This exercise takes two partners.

Step 1: write for seven minutes. This is a scene from the past in which your innocence is lost or trust is broken. Recall that moment in all its detail, using the senses to describe it. At the same time, your writing partner writes a similar paragraph about their own lives.

Step 2: swap stories.

It's now your job to respond to that person's story with another narrative of your own. Your response is made up of acknowledgement of their experience as well as your own sharing. Pay attention to the words you use, the images you evoke.

You have just created a literary event – a piece of collective memoir.

Shaimaa

I don't know exactly when my urge to 'run away' became a life's goal. It could've been sometime during my childhood when I found out that my parents were not invincible and that, sooner or later, I would have to make my own way in life. Or maybe it was during puberty when my body and the world turned on me …

If the systematic will to kill a spirit and strip a human being of their value and individuality was ever declared a crime as deplorable and punishable as murder, then women in my region, and arguably the world over, would be survivors of a genocide. Imagination was the safest place I had and, with it, the power to disappear in broad daylight.

*

I've become really good at disappearing. At making myself small and invisible. You learn to perfect that if you're a woman growing up in the Middle East. Shelley, you put it so well one time: 'It's like you suddenly turn off your magnetic field.' I retreated within myself. But that came at a cost I thought I was happy to pay. …

2.

Shelley

The university of Qatar was built on the idea, I learned from a colleague, that if a thief came onto the premises, he would get lost. So, classroom 224 might be next door to 136, and 441 might be next to 39. The most stressful part of the day was finding the room I was to teach in. It was in one of these rooms that we met, you and I.

*

Every morning I awoke, and I thought, 'I am in Doha, Qatar, on the Arabian Gulf'. I looked out into the humid, purple-blue air, over dust and rubble towards the Corniche, and beyond that, towards the shallow turquoise waters of the Gulf where once in 1991, according to a rumour, an errant missile sent by Saddam Hussein and meant for Saudi Arabia, had landed. It had exploded, killing fish and making a hole in the soft seabed.

(Davidow & Khalil 2022: 2–6)

I believe we all have good stories. It does, though, take work and craft and skill to tell those well. When working and writing with others, as I've shown, part of the process is that we each allow the unique 'voice' of the other writer/s to emerge – and that we work with the messy tapestry of life as we attempt the challenge of a cohesive 'whole'. The following exercise also requires a writing partner.

EXERCISE: *Before you left ...*

Write a poem of 10–13 lines to your writing partner. If you are writing alone, you can write to anyone you choose.

Write in iambic pentameter – as in the example above – 10 syllables for each line, begin with an unstressed syllable. There is no rhyme. Start with the word 'be**fore**,' which is unstressed, stressed.

It could begin like this: 'Before you left' or 'before we met' or 'before the accident'

Such as 'Before the accident I saw a wren ...' (10 syllables, stressed, unstressed – Shakespeare wrote in iambic pentameter – very frequently in his plays).

Problems with collective memoirs

Autobiography and memoir, as Lejeune defines them, are one person's account of themselves. But if we bring in another author, another narrator, another protagonist, how will this work? Do the two (or more voices) alternate, weave, respond to each other or not? In the case of two authors, do they consult before they write, during and after? Do they modify their memoirs to accommodate the other? How do they negotiate theme? These problems have no single answer. The process of creating a collective memoir is a radical one and as Paul's account illuminates, is as unique to the relationship being reflected as your own singular memoir is to you as a person.

Paul

Recently I wrote a collective memoir with one other person. It was a baring of two souls and how we interconnected, even though we were from very different cultures, genders, race, religions, countries, hemispheres. She would write a section, for example, about her experience of growing up in her culture, and I would give my account of how it was to grow up in mine, and then we would comment on each other's work, creating a conversation. Her memoir became a confession addressed not to a reader but to me, and likewise my confession was addressed to her. This was fruitful because it kept us honest and responsive to what truths we needed to explore. At some points, she would write – *are you just writing that because you don't want to offend me? What do you really think?* What was remarkable, however, was that even though we had two very different stories, two individual memoirs, combined, the whole was more than the parts, and we found a third story emerging, one that had a separate voice, direction, a Hegelian synthesis emerging out of a thesis and anti-thesis.

The memoir was never published due to the offence it might cause others, but the exercise of writing together was a revelation, a catharsis, therapy, and enabled a deep understanding of ourselves.

In this chapter we have only given examples of dual-author memoir – two people writing together, but there is no reason why a group of people could not write a memoir – three, ten, twenty, a community. It would be interesting to see what such a collective memoir would be like.

Conclusion

The potential of the collective memoir to shift the concept of what memoir is has barely been tapped. We all know that there is beauty but also perhaps danger in the single narrative. There is perhaps even more beauty (and risk) in a collective narrative.

Any narrative that purports to be 'true' puts the weight of the responsibility of 'truth' on the writer to be accurate – to maintain fidelity to emotional truth, whatever that may be – is our job. The devil is in the detail. How do we do this?

Once a single story is held by two or more voices, it becomes much more than the sum total of its parts – it becomes radical. Each memoir is unique. Each collective is unique. There is no formula and no downloadable template for the radical collective memoir.

To use a musical metaphor, the collective memoir offers the writer and the reader the melody and the harmony and the counterpoint. To expand the musical metaphor this form could be seen as the equivalence of a fugue: the literary value lies in the resonance between sections. In a fugue, a theme is played, repeated, taken up, re-interpreted and changed as the piece goes along. In the collective memoir, two or maybe more writers might take up a theme, play with it – each voice interpreting that theme in its own unique way, so that the 'truth' emerges as something multi-faceted, potentially even contradictory. We know that the measure of good literature is in its artistic merit, but it is also in how that work moves us, leaves us changed, richer, deeper. After reading a breathtakingly good book, such as the novel (which is really a biography/memoir) *Apeirogon* (McCann 2020), the reader cannot look at the world in exactly the same way afterwards.

Good books sharpen and change our perception. The collective memoir has the capacity, I believe, to expand the territory of the genre. Memoir writers, as they set out to show 'what really happened', can take readers into a place of many-sidedness, where one voice is counterpointed by another in a combined narrative that illuminates the truths we tell in new and profound ways.

9

Autrebiography

In the early chapters of this book, we discussed how memoir is, in Lejeune's words, 'a retrospective prose narrative produced by a real person concerning his [*sic*] own existence, focusing on his [*sic*] individual life, in particular on the development of his [*sic*] personality' (Lejeune 1989: 2).[1] For memoir and autobiography not to cross the line into fiction, 'the author, the narrator and the protagonist must be identical' (Lejeune 1989: 4). In other words, the reader trusts that the author whose name is on the cover of the book is the same person who is narrating the life story and the first-person protagonist is also the same person, and that this person is 'one single stable identity'. If we separate this trinity, we are no longer writing memoir.

But Roland Barthes, the French semiologist and literary theorist, disagrees. He claims that it is a fallacy to equate author, narrator and protagonist whom he insists can never be one and the same person. Following Derrida's ideas, the past self, says Barthes, is a fictional 'other', a 'text' to be read, and the writing of memoir is actually the reading of the past self as a text. He also suggests that the past self is a powerless victim in the hands of a present dictator, the author, who determines exactly how our past self is read.

An example of a memoir that plays with these ideas is Dave Eggers's *A Heartbreaking Work of Staggering Genius* (2001), where in a long preface, the author argues that the younger self he is writing about is made up, and that he has written over and destroyed a delicate and complex history of early years by writing his memoir: 'This was me then, and I can look at that person, from the distance I now have, and throw water balloons on his stupid fat head' (Eggers 2001: iii).

---

[1]This chapter and the next one are based on an article published in *TEXT* on 'Autrebiography' (2019).

Eggers admits that his narrator self in the present with all his supposed wisdom and experience takes the moral high ground and imposes his arrogant, dismissive view of his past 'self', based on the so-called superior vantage point of the present time. Instead of portraying 'the past', Eggers admits that he has retroactively clothed his past self in twenty-first-century fashion.

I know this to be true in my own writing experience. Although I think of myself in the past as the same person as I am now, sometimes as I write about this younger self, I do not recognize him as me. I sometimes read his letters in amazement, thinking – who was this person? A stranger. If I met him on the street, would I even recognize him? Would he recognize me? I also know that by writing about him, I am speaking over him, replacing him with my modern-day version of who I think he was, creating a story about him that may not be him, and his powerless to stop me erasing his life. *Soldier Blue*, for example, gave a picture of my younger self which I would like to revise, rewrite, perhaps try to give him more say, if that were possible.

Breaking the reader/writer contract

This reader/writer contract is the essence of memoir and it is this contract to which readers hold authors accountable: readers expect that authors are telling the truth, and that the trinity of author/narrator/protagonist is one.

This chapter will challenge both of those assumptions about writing memoir.

As we have seen in an earlier chapter, language does not describe the world as it is and does not portray the 'truth' of this world. Philosopher Immanuel Kant (2004) distinguished between the unknowable world – the thing-in-itself (*das Ding an sich*) and our understanding or experience of the world through our senses, the way that thing-it-itself appears to an observer. We can only describe in language, which is not the world: 'language should not directly name or identify truth which would make it a form of identity logic, but surround truth' (Lee 2005: 64). If this is true, then writing memoir is an impossible task, the reader/writer contract is impossible to uphold, and memoir becomes a subjective recalling of a present construction of the past through language which can only reflect our modern ways of seeing, not describe the past as it really was. We cannot accurately say 'what really happened' or represent the past in retrospective prose: 'it is through language that we create the world ... we do not describe the world we see, but we see the world we describe' (Jaworski 1996: 178).

Secondly, when we as authors write about ourselves as protagonists or speak as narrators, these are not the same 'person'. The 'I' in a memoir is a persona who substitutes for, and displaces, the living writer (de Man 1979: 919). The protagonist is a fictional construction who cannot be the author who is outside the text, writing it. The story that the author writes about this protagonist cannot be the truth about themselves or even what happened to themselves. The 'reader/writer contract' the author has implicitly made with the reader is broken the moment the 'author' writes a word on the page about their 'self'. Even if the author simply records 'facts' about themselves, the act of writing is a process of selection of facts used, which are discarded, which are prioritized. And the contract is broken the moment a writer chooses one 'fact' over the other.

> Autobiography is a kind of self-writing in which you are constrained to respect the facts of your history. But which facts? All the facts? No. All the facts are too many facts. You choose the facts insofar as they fit in with your evolving purpose.
>
> (Coetzee 1992: 18)

Autrebiography

There is a name for this. In an interview with David Atwell in 2006, the author J. M. Coetzee coined the term '*autre*biography' for a narrative that separates the author from the narrator and protagonist. Whereas autobiography (literally self-biography-writing) equates all three, autrebiography (literally other-biography-writing) suggests that the protagonist is not the author. In this chapter, we will examine how J. M. Coetzee's series of 'autobiographical' works, *Scenes from Provincial Life*, published under the titles *Boyhood* (1997), *Youth* (2002) and *Summertime* (2009), sets out to deliberately break the reader/ writer contract in two ways: separating author, narrator and protagonist by using the third person, and casting doubts on the reliability of memory to gain access to the truth of the past.

> David Atwell: (interviewer): When one tries to put the historical self into writing, what emerges, inevitably, is a substitute for that self. Would you agree that at a basic representational level, all autobiography is *autre*biography? If so, is your decision to write autobiography in the third person a case of making this process explicit?
>
> J. M. Coetzee: Yes, all autobiography is *autre*biography, but what is more important is where one goes from there. With regard to my own practice, I can only say that to rewrite *Boyhood* or *Youth* with 'I' substituted for 'he' throughout would leave you with two books only remotely related to their originals. This is an astonishing fact, yet any reader can confirm it within a few pages.
>
> (Coullie et al 2006: 216)

*Autre*biography then demonstrates the Barthesian idea that the author when writing about a past self is reading/interpreting that self, and further is writing about another person who is not the author. Perhaps the author is also the narrator of this other self, but that is also questionable.

EXERCISE: *An astonishing fact – autrebiography*

Write a paragraph of 200 words about an incident that happened more than ten years ago, using 'I' (first person). Then rewrite the same passage in the third person. Note the difference and distance this creates. Which one do you prefer? Which one reflects the emotional truth of the incident better? Keep that one.

Unflinchingness

J. M. Coetzee's *Boyhood*, the first book of his autobiographic trilogy, is an exercise in 'unflinchingness', in other words, looking objectively and critically at his younger self, the protagonist, without romanticizing the past or this 'boyhood'. For J. M. Coetzee, childhood is not 'a time of innocent joy', but rather 'a time of gritting the teeth and enduring' Coetzee 1998: 14).

> It's a good thing that we should grow fond of the self we once were … we should not be too strict with our child selves … Nevertheless, we can't wallow in comfortable wonderment at our past. We must see what the child, still befuddled from his travels, still trailing his clouds of glory, could not see … Forgivingness but also unflinchingness: that is the mixture I have in mind, if it is attainable. First the unflinchingness, then the forgivingness.
>
> (Coetzee 1998: 29)

The author separates himself from his child self, deconstructs him, as he sets himself the task of 'unravelling contradictions in the context of a culturally racially conflicted society' (Jacobs 2011: 43).

> He knows that he is damaged. He has a sense that something is slowly tearing inside him all the time: a wall, a membrane. He tries to hold himself as tight as possible to keep the tearing within bound. To keep it within bounds, not to stop it: nothing will stop it.
>
> (Coetzee 1998: 9)

Paul

The advantage that we have over our past selves is that we have hindsight and historical context that our younger selves did not. So maybe we should not judge them too harshly. A number of legal cases have emerged recently of people who are tried for crimes they did in the past, and we need to be cognizant of different cultural norms and systems out of which those crimes arose. Do we punish a former headmaster now for caning schoolchildren back in the sixties? Do I condemn my parents for blowing smoke into my face when I was a baby? The wisdom of hindsight can lead to a judgemental moral high ground, and we have to take into consideration the context of our past life when analysing it.

As I describe in the last chapter, my memoir *Soldier Blue* chronicles my life growing up in a racist and colonial society where at the time I (he) was unaware of my limited view of the world. Only later when writing the memoir did I see my younger self as arrogant and narrow. I could then write an 'unflinching' portrayal of that self which became an ironic exposé of previous attitudes.

> I had to carry the sad burden of having liberal parents. How could they not vote for Ian Smith? Hadn't they learned? I remonstrated with them, even showed them the Albert Schweitzer quote we had laboriously copied down from the geography teacher's board: *There is something that all white men who have lived here, must learn and know; that these individuals are a sub-race; they have neither the intellectual, mental or emotional abilities to equate or share in any of the functions of our civilisation.*
>
> (Williams 2008: 75)

Shelley

My immigrant memoir *The Eye of the Moon* (2007) is written in episodic sections where the past and present (Africa and America) are juxtaposed. This gives me the opportunity to mirror in the text, temporal and geographic dislocation reflected in the separation of the narrator in the future looking back at a younger more confident, even arrogant self with judgement laced to some degree, with envy.

> The issue is always money. I don't have any. I can't find a job even waitressing because the waiting list for such positions is endless. And the people who work in restaurants have degrees, in Science or Drama or Botany. There are no jobs for them in their fields.

After I return from Cape Town my family takes out a loan against their house, and I go to university. I work hard and realize that the Muse who inspired Keats, Wordsworth, Shelley is redundant. I cannot get beyond a C, because I will not look on Caliban as the Colonized and Prospero as the archetypal Colonizer in Shakespeare Against Apartheid. Instead Apartheid is in itself according to me an enactment of some bitter archetype.

In retrospect I detect in myself an almost arrogant unwillingness to take part in the university era of my life. As though I somehow thought myself beyond it.

(Davidow 2007: 11)

EXERCISE: *Unflinchingness*

Write a 300-word paragraph about an incident in your teens. Somewhere in the piece present a reflection as per the examples above, on the distance between that past self and the present self who is now writing the paragraph. Be as 'unflinching' as you can. But be forgiving too!

Autobiografiction

A radical memoir may also blur the boundaries of fiction and fact, or at least needs to question those boundaries. J. M. Coetzee tells David Atwell in the interview referred to above, that 'all writing is autobiography' (Coetzee 1992: 17).

Getting to the core of yourself may not be feasible ... perhaps the best you can hope for will not be the history of yourself but a story about yourself, a story that will not be the truth but may have some truth-value, probably of a mixed kind – some historical, some poetic truth. A fiction of the truth in other words.

(Coetzee 1999)

Paul de Man, similarly in 'Autobiography as de-facement', suggests that fiction is disguised autobiography, and the converse might also be true: autobiography, memoir, life writing, is fiction.

EXERCISE: *Truth or lie*

Write three things about yourself, one of which is a lie (a fiction). Share with a partner or writing group and ask them to guess which is the truth (autobiography) and which is the lie (the fiction). Make the lie about yourself as convincing as possible.

Derrida asks us to be suspicious of hard and fast binaries – true/false, good/ evil, Black/white, male/female and it is the same with the binaries we have constructed around autobiography and memoir. Perhaps there is a grey area between fiction/non-fiction that radical memoir can explore. Such instability, such paradox, makes memoir interesting. And by challenging these assumptions, we are in good company.

In *Self Impression: Life-Writing, Autobiografiction, and the Forms of Modern Literature* (2010), Max Saunders calls such binaries – fiction/non-fiction, fiction/memoir – unstable, and prefers the term 'autobiografiction' that embraces both binaries: he argues that the boundaries between autobiography and fiction have always been unstable. The narrator of *One Flew over the Cuckoo's Nest* claims that 'it's the truth even if it didn't happen' (Kesey 1962: 13); Philip Roth suggests that also undermines the simple binaries of truth and fiction by stating that 'memoirs lie and fiction tells the truth' (Drabble 2010: 110); J. M. Coetzee celebrates this instability:

> Everything that you write, including criticism and fiction, writes you as you write it. The real question is: This massive autobiographical writing-enterprise that fills a life, the enterprise of self-construction … does it yield only fictions? Or rather, among the fictions of the self, the versions of the self, that it yields, are there any truer than others? How do I know when I have the truth about myself?
>
> (Coetzee 1992: 17)

Barthes plays with the notion of writer as reader of the self as other; Coetzee plays with many counter-selves (see below); Nabokov refracts a writer self into doubled and mirrored characters, and contemporary writers attempting autobiography are freed to play the game of 'self-construction' (Nabokov 1990: 23).

Critics of J. M. Coetzee's trilogy of autrebiographies were perturbed at his Autobiografictions. *Boyhood*, *Youth* and *Summertime* are part autobiography and part fiction, and contain deliberate 'factual inaccuracies'. In *Boyhood*, Coetzee has changed some historical names (Attridge 2004: 149) and in *Youth* there are some glaring incongruities and obvious 'non-facts', for example, the protagonist is single, yet it is common knowledge that Coetzee was married at that time. J. M. Coetzee 'has woven fictional episodes into a framework of autobiography' (Attridge 2004: 160). The question is why? Why deliberately falsify facts about your past?

EXERCISE: *Autobiografiction*

Write a 300-word paragraph about yourself that may or may not be true. Or it may have some truth. It could be a story someone else has told about you, or one you invented, a lie you told once about yourself. You can also add a reflection on how this self and story has been constructed.

'How do I know when I have the truth about myself?' J. M. Coetzee asks. 'What is the truth about oneself? Perhaps that memoirs expose the grand lie that the 'truth' is but a 'fiction of the truth' (Coetzee 1992: 17).

Autobiographics

Barthes has shown us how we can separate author from protagonist, that the self is actually another person, and J. M. Coetzee illustrates this in *Boyhood* and *Youth*. But can we now separate the author from the narrator of a memoir? The narrator is often the invisible voice of the author, and the reader will inevitably assume that the 'I' of the narrator is the author. But is it possible to separate author from narrator? Who is telling the story of yourself? Does it necessarily have to be you the author? Could it be someone else?

If you write about someone else's life, we call it biography. But is it possible to write a biography about yourself? If you become another narrator and write about you as an 'other' 'self', then you are writing autobiographics.

Leigh Gilmore coined the term 'autobiographics' (1992) and splits what we think of as a monolithic, ahistorical 'I' into a more nuanced and 'multiply coded' array of discourses (42). What she means by this is that what we assume is 'I' or the 'self' is not an unproblematic unified, timeless 'me' but needs to reflect 'the shifting sides of identity'. Autobiographics is Gilmore's feminist critique of what has been a static notion of autobiography written by a stable authorial disembodied and decontextualized 'self', whereas most people experience themselves as a changing, unstable field of 'interruptions and eruptions, with resistance and contradiction' (42). She offers strategies of self-representation that welcomes contradictions and multiple angles.

To apply this more practically, we should think of our 'self' not as one unchanging identity, but as sometimes a confusing array of multiple 'selves'. I could have easily written my memoir in several ways, describing different selves. It is good to acknowledge that we are not just a single unproblematic 'I', but need to write about the depth of our 'selves'.

Summertime is 'autobiographic' in this way as it contains 'polarised and discrepant interviews conducted with Coetzee's lovers, family and friends' as well as contradictory and often factually inaccurate narratives (Kusek 2012: 112). And interestingly, the author and narrator are not the same at all.

In *Summertime*, we discover that J. M. Coetzee is playing a game where it is impossible for the author to impose his view over his past life. In this 'autrebiography', 'J. M. Coetzee' (the 'author') is dead, and the book is a fragmentary collage of reminiscences and biographical investigation into the life of this author by others. There are several narrators who tell the story of the author, and they sometimes get it wrong. *Summertime* consists of fragmented entries of a notebook written by 'Coetzee', a series of interviews by an English biographer, Mr Vincent, whose task is to create a biography of the deceased author. Some of the interviews are clearly inaccurate, biased, unflinching and disparage more than glorify the dead author. *Summertime* is more of a parody of an autobiography, and deconstructs the assumptions made about memoir and the reader/writer contract. The *autre*-self is constructed not by the author this time, but out of the biased and unreliable accounts and memories of the people who supposedly knew J. M. Coetzee. Some of the accounts are not even complete and contain notes such as: 'To be expanded on'.

However unsettling this autobiographic, autobiografictional autrebiography is, it helps writers think of innovative ways we can tell our stories. It also unsettles the assumption that the author is in total control of their narrative. Why should we be the authority figure over our past selves and get to decide who they are and write over them, judge them, determine their identity?

Nabokov once wrote that he is the 'perfect dictator' over his characters and controls every thought every move of theirs (Nabokov 1990: 69). John Fowles, on the other hand, admitted (or his author persona in the novel) that he is the opposite. In *The French Lieutenant's Woman* (1969), the author loses control of his characters: 'I [the author] ordered him [the character] to walk straight back to Lyme Regis. But he gratuitously turned and went down to the Dairy' (Fowles 1992: 81). As authors of our memoirs, are we dictators of our past selves or do we relinquish control. Who do we allow to narrate their story?

Summertime takes autrebiography to an extreme. Not only is the protagonist separate from the author and narrator, his story has been hijacked and appropriated by the voices of others. Here, the self is a fiction constructed by others. J. M. Coetzee does not tell his own story, relinquishes authority both as author and narrator, and allows his story to be told by others, refracted and distorted through the lens of the methods biographers and autobiographers use to get to the 'truth'. And the truth we find in this book is not a fixed, monolithic series of 'facts', but constructed narratives/fictions, numerous versions of J. M. Coetzee's life. Whoever has power over the narrative gets to tell the 'truth'. History is told by the victors.

Paul

Here is the beginning of *Soldier Blue* where I describe my younger self biographically rather than autobiographically, told by a distant narrator who is not me. I try to get into his head and let him speak, not me:

At six o'clock on that same evening, a twenty-year-old white Rhodesian soldier sits on his arse on the banks of Lake Kariba, skimming stones into the weeds that choke the lake front. Crocodile eyes watch him across the surface of the water, and hippo noses blow bubbles at him. His weapon, an FN automatic, lies unloaded at his side. He watches the plane as long as his mind's eye can follow it, until it disappears gently in the dark night and becomes a star in the dusk, and the sound of its engines turns into screeching cicadas in the reeds. His story began innocently enough, but even in the beginning he sensed foreboding, futility, ineptitude. His parents had gone out to Africa, taking him with them on their adventure. They went to make something of themselves. But the seeds of his destiny were already sown in their smallest gestures, hesitations, and doubts.

(Williams 2008: 2)

Shelley

Below is a section from my biographical memoir *Whisperings in the Blood* (2016) where an objective narrator reflects on Shelley's childhood self in the autobiographic third person and tries to allow her space to speak for herself:

Some months later, the girl sits on the steps again, waiting. Mr Miller, the violin teacher, is late. She hopes he's forgotten about her lesson. She opens the violin case and pulls out the instrument chosen by her great-grandfather, the violinist. Long ago, thousands of kilometres away, his hands held this. She imagines him playing a scale on the three-quarter-size instrument in some shop, thinking about his grandson in Africa, thinking, Yes, this one sounds good.

Mr Miller's white sedan arrives. It's brown with dust from the dirt road. In the way he confidently straightens his collar, it can be seen that he is an excellent teacher who will make certain that she corrects her lazy hold on the violin, her too-tight grip on the bow, and her slow progress reading music. She stands up. Her heart empties. The notes she will play today will be harsh and scratchy and often out of tune. They will elicit criticism and shame. They will not do justice to such a fine instrument. They will not fill her with their beauty and illuminate the world. She doesn't know, as she stands there watching the teacher get his violin out of the back of his car, that this day will mark the end of months of lessons; that he will tell her he is wasting his time with her; that she will put the violin carefully back in its case and leave it untouched for the next thirty years.

(Davidow 2016: 7)

EXERCISE: *Autobiographics*

Write a selection of short pieces about yourself as if narrated by a lover, a friend, an old teacher, your nemesis. Show yourself from another point of view or from several points of view. Let someone else narrate your memoir!

The aim here is to describe your self or selves as a multiplicity of discourses, 'interruptions and eruptions, with resistance and contradiction as strategies of self-representation'.

Have fun!

Conclusion

Of course we cannot really let our past self speak if we are writing them, unless we can find a time-travelling DeLorean and literally visit our past selves. But it is good to realize that they lived in another time, place, and to respect them, try to understand them, allow them a voice, not throw water balloons at their 'fat head'. Often we can find their voice, their personality, in their diaries, letters or mementoes, and these may help us reconstruct their identities.

It is also worth reading the J. M. Coetzee trilogy of autrebiographies to see how he has trodden carefully as a present-day memoirist and allowed his past selves to speak, or (in the case of the last book of the trilogy) how present selves talk over and erase his past self. The devices he uses help us write radical memoirs that get to the root of who we are, who we were, how we create a record of ourselves, how we write: 'I was here!'

10

Biographemes

Lyotard's grand and petit récits

When we write a memoir, we often try to give the big picture, tell a grand narrative that encompasses everything about us. What we are trying to do is maybe unconsciously write autobiography. But writing a grand narrative is not only impossible: it is dishonest. We cannot possibly write the whole story of our lives, and if we think we have, we have simply given one story, one angle and passed it off as truth.

Jean-François Lyotard (1924–98) was a French philosopher who coined the terms 'grand récit' and 'petit récit'. The 'grand narratives' or 'grand récits' are stories we tell ourselves that claim to explain everything, that give a monolithic view of events, people's lives, and exclude other points of view. A grand narrative, he claims, is a type of cultural myopia and we find it in fundamentalist religions, political ideologies of the left and right. He cites a few – such as Marxism and Capitalism – that claim an all-encompassing world view.

Lyotard prefers 'petits récits' or 'little narratives' that give specific here and now stories or fragments rather than generalized overviews. We do not know everything, even about our own lives, so to try to encompass a whole view of our life in memoir or autobiography is simply not possible, and we should be suspicious of anyone who claims to give a true and objective and accurate and ideological account of their lives. *Petits récits* have no such claim to universal truth status.

This seems to contradict our advice in earlier chapters where we asked you to look for a large pattern in your life, such as the hero's journey or a Freytag's pyramid structure, or some other 'grand narrative' to make sense of your life and to follow that pattern in your memoir. But often by imposing a grand scheme or pattern on our lives, we do not reflect our experiences accurately. Our lives are also made up of small incidents that do not fit neatly into the idea of what we think our lives are or should be or should have been.

They simply are.

In the graph we asked you to map, there are patterns of rise and fall that may inform the memoir. In real life, of course, there are also unexplained events, anomalies, contradictions, things that don't fit the theme, if we find one, idiosyncrasies that point to the cracks and silences and gaps in our lives. These may tell us more about who we are than what we think we know.

Paul

Here is a 'petit récit' I included in *Soldier Blue*. It is not part of the grand narrative and serves to fragment the narrative, and at the time of writing I did not understand its significance, but felt it was something essential, some little side story that needed to go in there.

> On a weekend pass through Bulawayo, McKechnie (a fellow medic) and I strolled around town on a Saturday morning. We fell in line behind two giggling women who had noticed us and were passing comments about 'handsome uniforms'. We followed them up and down the streets, and they led us on, escorting us through Haddon & Sly, Woolworth's, in and out of the lingerie section of Greatermans, and finally to a Wimpy restaurant in Grey Avenue. We were meant to follow them in, sit down and order them a drink of coffee, and begin chatting, flirting, and 'scoring'. But McKechnie said he had to be back at barracks, and I marched fiercely past the restaurant, willing myself to walk in, but unable to.
>
> (Williams 2008: 223)

The incident is never followed up in the rest of the book, never connected to anything else, or commented on, and is left hanging. I can see now why I included it, because it is a 'petit récit', a small fragment of my past life that the older narrator cannot make sense of or fit into the 'grand narrative' but is a necessary component of his being.

EXERCISE: *Petit récit*

Write a 300-word anecdote, fragment, or small incident from your life that stands alone. It may not fit in with any theme you have uncovered. Maybe it does not even make sense to you, but it happened and it has some significance.

Barthes's biographemes

Imagine a memoir that is not a grand narrative at all, not a hero's journey, not shaped by Freytag's pyramid of your graph of rise and fall, not shaped by the author or present self. Imagine a memoir that is simply a collection of memories, stories, fragments, 'petits récits' like the example above. How would your memoir look?

Roland Barthes by Roland Barthes (1977) is such a memoir. It comprises ninety-two narratives, arranged alphabetically, not chronologically, which he calls a 'circle of fragments'. He has collected ninety-two 'petits récits', stories, fragments, photographs, mementoes, that are not organized into one cohesive 'grand narrative' or shaped by the present-day writing self. By putting them alphabetically, he is deliberately trying to avoid the 'author' imposing meaning on his past life, but rather presents his memoir as a set of random memories. In this way, Barthes tries to make sure that the present self does not have 'the last word' and dictate what his younger self was like, does not impose a grand narrative on him, avoids what he calls a tyranny of the present over the past. Barthes calls these 'petits récits' 'biographemes', or 'the short note, the brief sketch' (Barthes 1975: 189), and he wrote these fragments on index cards. These cards were not in any particular order and could be shuffled around. His life 'texts' are 'disjointed, no one of them caps any other' (189).

Furthermore, these biographemes are marginal. He calls them 'aslant', 'interpolations', 'parentheses' (Barthes 1977: 73) explaining that 'writing must go hand in hand with silence', and that 'the author never produces anything but presumptions of meaning, forms, and it is the world which fills them' (Barthes 1972: xi).

EXERCISE: *Biographemes*

Write three 'biographemes', three short 100-word 'petits récits' that are unrelated memories. These could be anecdotes, fragments or small incidents from your life that stand alone. Put them in random order.

Roland Barthes's 'biographemes' are also experimental in form. They are not all prose narratives. They are transmedial. Some are poems, some are photographs, some are 'to do' lists, doodles, signatures. These are all 'memoirs' of his past self, and he is not going to narrate the story or string it all together, but rather let the reader make sense of these disjointed fragments. Biographemes are radical not just because they are 'petits récits' but because of their innovative form. They do not have to be written narratives in a conventional sense but any snapshots or fragments of your life. A photo can be a biographeme (like the photo you wrote about in Chapter 1), or a *Haiku*, or an anecdote, or anything that gives us an insight into who you are.

EXERCISE: *Transmedia*

Add to your 'biographemes' and the first 'petit récit' you wrote some fragments of your past self, such as a photograph, an old letter, a text message, a drawing you did as a child. Rearrange these fragments in random order to make a collage of your past self that others can read.

This can be fun, but it serves a serious purpose, to let your younger past self speak without you speaking on top of them. This collage of biographemes allows a silence between the narratives, a space between each, and what happens in the implied and the unwritten give the reader a chance to see into the 'dark matter' that lives between the lines.

> What I write about myself is never the last word … my texts are disjointed, no one of them caps any other; the latter is nothing but a further text, the last in the series but not the ultimate in meaning … What right does my present have to speak of my past? Has my present some advantage over my past?
>
> (Barthes 1977: 120)

Barthes reinforces what we mentioned earlier: people have a 'different knowledge today than yesterday' (Barthes 1977: 120). What we piece together now as grand narrative is nothing more than discontinuous memory-images or what he calls 'phantasmatics' (Barthes 1977: 153). What Roland Barthes does in his memoir is break the idea of a retrospective narrative about a continuous and contiguous self called Roland Barthes, but instead offers a series of competing constructions with equal power over their meaning. The act of writing memoir for Barthes is an act of reading the past Roland Barthes as text with all its codes and Lacanian mirror images.

Barthes is not the only writer to use biographemes to give the reader 'petits récits' that tell the stories of our life rather than 'the story' of our life. Walter Benjamin's *One-way Street* (1928), for example, is a modernist mosaic of disconnected 'biographemes' present as random memory fragments of a person's impression of Weimar in the 1920s. These snapshots vary in form, play with different voices and styles, and imitate the way memory is stored and retrieved. Similarly, Richard Wirick's *One Hundred Siberian Postcards* (2006) contains a hundred short memory fragments, or glimpses of story arranged as 'postcards' so the reader creates the whole picture by patching the 'petits récits' together, filling in the gaps. Wirick argues that this is how memory works, not as a continuous organized grand narrative but as random, episodic snippets that need to be threaded together.

Using third person: the self as other, or the other as self

In *Soldier Blue*, as I have said earlier, I had a wiser narrator tell the story of the naive younger Paul Williams, to guide us as readers into this younger Paul's world. But the older narrator also makes judgements over his early figure, selects what was important and what is left out. What if the younger self is allowed free rein to tell his own story? Would he tell a different one?

J. M. Coetzee uses the third person to describe an 'other' self and Barthes similarly alternates between first and third person to distance himself from his younger self. 'I had no other solution than to rewrite myself – at a distance, a great distance – here and now' (Barthes 1975: 142). To write in the third person about oneself, as Barthes does, is not new. Andrei Codrescu's *The Life and Times of an Involuntary Genius*, for example, uses the third person in order to create distance and in order to view the 'self under construction' (Codrescu 1994: 24). Lejeune argues that when an author chooses to use third person, 'he pretends to speak about himself as someone else might ... or invent[s] a fictive narrator to present the author's point of view or tell his life story' (Lejeune 1977: 27) without breaking what he calls the 'autobiographic pact' (author = narrator = protagonist). But to use the third person in order to make the point that the 'self' written about is 'other', that is, is not the author, appears to overturn this very premise.

Shelley's *Eye of the Moon* is a memoir, but it is written in alternate first (I), second (you) and third person (the girl). It is also a series of very short vignettes not told chronologically. The effect of this is to allow readers to see her past life from many angles, not just as a grand narrative told by an all-wise narrator.

At seventeen, I am selfish, taking him, this forty-six-year-old, for myself.

*

And then one day you left. For America. This was after The Journalist. There was no way of making money. You had fallen in love with someone else.

*

The girl said, my mother nearly died, oh the phone to the grandmother –
she felt proud that the mother had not died …

(Davidow 2007: 4–6)

This may be something you try in your memoir – alternating first, second,
third-person point of view, giving fragments of your life, fractured memories
rather than one long, organized sweep of smooth narrative. This may help
dethrone the absolute dictator, the present 'I' who is telling the story.

Méconnaissance

Radical memoir questions everything including the idea of a continuous self.
Swedish molecular biologist Dr Jonas Frisen discovered that a human body's
cells replace themselves every seven to ten years. The philosophical question
then is this: are we the same person if every single cell of our body is not
the same as it was ten years ago? Genetically, our DNA is transferred to the
new cells, so we do not become different people in essence, but it is worth
considering that we do change physically and psychologically over the years. So
how then can we write about our former selves which have changed so much?

One of the oldest thought experiments is the Ancient Greek paradox of
Theseus' ship, told by Heraclitus and Plato some 500 years BCE. The story goes
like this: Theseus took a trip across the seas, and in the years he was away, he
had to replace all the parts of the ship as they wore out or broke. Theseus and
his sailors had to replace the sail, the mast, every single wooden plank that
made up the ship, every nail, every bolt. So when he returned to port, the ship
looked the same but physically it was not the same ship at all. Now let's say a
thief followed the ship on its journey and took very old part that was discarded
and made a new ship out of these parts. Now there are two ships. Which one
is the actual genuine ship?

The allegory is clear – are we the same person we were ten years ago, twenty
years ago? We have replaced our cells, our thinking, our world views, we have
changed our minds, learned new things, grown physically and mentally. We
cannot assume that when we say 'I' meaning our past self, that this 'I' is the
same person we are now.

The psychologist Jacques Lacan (1901–81) suggests that the 'self' is not a stable subject, and is fictively constructed of language, and even pre-linguistically: when a baby sees itself in a mirror, it constructs the (false) notion of the self as a 'whole, unified body', a misrecognition, or '*méconnaissance*') (Lacan 2001: 1285). To misconstrue or misrecognize is an easy thing. Outside our house is a magpie lark who keeps thinking it sees another bird in the reflective glass of the pool fence, and pecks at it, chirps at it and flaps its wings in annoyance when it pecks and chirps back. This is an instance of *méconnaissance*. Lacan maintains that we do the same with the idea of our 'self'. It is an illusion. Throughout our lives, our 'ego' holds on to the idea of an autonomous, unchanging self, but for Lacan, this mistaken 'self' is shaped by its relation to others, by the desires of others, by social expectations and prohibitions (or as Freud calls them, the superego and id). Our 'self' is not a simple static entity that exists outside of the world and interacts with it.

J. M. Coetzee in his autrebiographies, periautobiographies and autobiografictions, and Barthes in his biographemes write memoirs that take Lacan's idea of this misrecognized illusion that there is a 'whole, unified self'. The 'I' is neither a fixed past self we can describe objectively, nor is the author or narrator 'I' a stable fixed entity hovering above our past experience and dictating who we are or were, but what Lacan calls an 'ego' built with the pre-existing Lego blocks of language and through our relations with others. We are a pastiche of perceptions 'infected' by language, and if we are to write an accurate memoir about our 'self' we have to deconstruct these grand narratives about ourselves and write about the fragments of self we are, how others see us, how we are determined by our language, culture and its rules and taboos.

EXERCISE: *Méconnaissance*

Imagine you are attending your own funeral. What would others say about you? Write a few short paragraphs, each one by an imagined friend, family member, work colleague and allow for contradiction in this pastiche. The selves written about may be misconstrued, but they show that we are not a unified self, that we change and that we are circumscribed by the views of those who shape us as we grow.

Writing a memoir then, according to Barthes, is an activity where 'the subject unmakes himself, like a spider dissolving in the constructive secretions of its web' (Barthes 1975: 64). A radical memoir will recognize that the 'self' is not (in Lacan's words), a 'unified subject'. J. M. Coetzee similarly will write a memoir such as *Summertime* where the self he writes about is constructed by others. We often find this at a funeral, where the speeches, eulogies construct a picture of the deceased that is not always accurate. Derrida has a word for this – he calls it 'autothanatography', memoir written by an author who is already dead (Derrida 1998: 49). J. M. Coetzee's *Summertime* is a literal example of this.

Autothanatography: Autrebiographic strategies for writers

Maybe we can rewrite the reader/writer contract to encompass these ideas – yes, when we write our memoir, we must be honest, open and true, but to do this we should not overwrite our younger selves with a dictatorial authorial or narrator tyranny or a single narrative. We need to surrender the control of the meaning of our texts, must not impose a grand narrative and let our former selves speak in 'petits récits', let the readers create meaning, maybe become readers of our younger selves and not determiners or authors of meaning. We need to 'depose the author from his or her central place as the source of meaning and undermined the unified subject of autobiography' (Anderson 2011: 6).

By surrendering the power of the author, exposing the way we have constructed our grand narratives, we allow the younger self to 'speak', to emerge, as an 'autre'.

How would such a memoir look? In the following exercise we ask you to gather all the fragments of selves, all the exercise you have written as you have worked through this book and collect them in one big portfolio of 'petits récits'. Maybe call it by your name: *Paul Williams* by Paul Williams. *Shelley Davidow* by Shelley Davidow. Mine would include the photo in chapter, the break-up letter, all the stories I have given as examples in this book, and more – a recording of me as an eleven-year-old, learning to play the ukulele, the graphs of my happiness index, and girls I loved as a teenager, my first stories written as a child, newspaper clippings of me, an old bad school report saying I would never be good at English, etc.

Conclusion

Throughout this book we have offered a number of writing exercises that may help you write your memoir. Some may have helped you directly; others may have been more to help you with the skills needed to go and write your memoir. We asked you at the beginning of the book to attempt them all and keep them in a folder, because if you have, then you have already written a radical memoir and all you need to complete it is to collate these exercises and put them in one file, following on from each other. All these exercises put together comprise ways of writing about yourself that reveal aspects of yourself and your past. All you need to do is collate these exercises in whatever order you wish, make them into a book of some sort – either printed or an eBook, and you have your radical memoir.

EXERCISE: *Portfolio – your radical memoir*

Collect and collate all the exercises in this book, including the photographs, graphs, experimental forms, poetry, etc., and create a portfolio of these fragments. Arrange them in whatever order you want, format them. Give the memoir a title. Perhaps you now have a first draft.

Afterword: Your radical memoir

Writing a radical memoir means writing as an unfettered and unique self, bringing your story to light with the awareness that the 'truth' of what happened depends on the interpreter of that truth doing their best to convey the feeling of 'what it was like from my point of view'.

The radical memoir requires the writer to be brutally honest whilst being aware that the truth *I* tell about an event may not be the truth you'd tell, even if we were both there. The radical memoir questions everything, every assumption about who we are and the truths we tell. The world around us has to be translated into words, and those words matter – and the more skilled the writer becomes, the more the words disappear, until all that's left in the heart of a reader is the story, its beauty, its ability to move the reader, change the reader.

It's also likely evident that by now you, the writer, have changed.

Writing ourselves into existence changes us. Writing this memoir book changed us as authors, as people. It sharpened us, allowed us to gather together our combined decades of wisdom, and write a handbook, an academic book, a collective memoir about our individual experiences living and writing about living. We have learned a lot along the way through writing.

Hopefully that meta-aspect of the book shows you that the radical memoir might appear in disguise – its content masquerading under other clothes, in another form – in this case, as a handbook/textbook/academic book/personal reflective piece of creative non-fiction.

Shelley

The radical memoir exists in any form you need it to take. Colum McCann called *Apeirogon* a novel, even though the stories and accounts are completely true. The main characters in the book are real men who have entrusted their stories to McCann and who work with him to counter hatred and the division between Jews and Palestinians. Both of the men in the book lost their young daughters to violence perpetrated by the opposite side. There are no untrue words in the whole book. Yes, perhaps sometimes there are good reasons to write a radical memoir and call it a novel. It releases the writer from the reader/writer contract. Even if it's true, no one is going to hold you to account, or tell you, hey, that didn't really happen like that – because it's a novel. You can say whatever you want. A radical memoir could be a prose-poem, a series of poems, a story written by more than one person. You could write your whole book in stream-of-consciousness or create your story or parts of it out of a collage of emails, newspaper clippings, letters, conversations. The form sometimes creates the content – and the impact. You are limited in form only as much as your imagination has limits. We encourage you to push boundaries and loosen the hold of the conventional ideas of what memoir 'should' be.

It shouldn't.
It can.
It could.
Be anything.
Play and discover.
Be fearless about failure.

There's no such thing anyway. Or perhaps everything is failure. Living in this world and writing about it is a journey in failure – a journey of endeavours, dreams, ideals that takes the writer to unanticipated places and generates unanticipated outcomes. That's the beauty of the journey – and the destination. As Thomas Edison once wrote: 'I have not failed. I have just found 10,000 ways that don't work' (Furr 2011: np). This is as true of art as of science. Trial and error. You have 10,000 opportunities to try things out. Hopefully, in this case as you seek to turn your life into art, you do in such a way that at some point you get to stand back and say, *wow, I think that works!*

Self-actualization and nakedness

It is unavoidable that to be 'true' you will expose the truth that the lines dividing fiction and memoir are blurred, that you question the assumption that telling the truth reveals (rather than conceals). And this is no easy road. It is littered with the burnt-out, the half-written, the almost-complete dreams that never materialized, of would-be memoir writers.

Virginia Woolf said that the reason so many memoirs are failures is that 'they leave out the person to whom things happened' (Woolf 1939: 1). As with life drawing, so with life writing: we expect nakedness. You can make a case for memoir being the most self-sacrificial of forms, the author laying herself open for the benefit of others who feel less alone in the world after reading it because an experience they've been through is articulated by someone else.

Leslie Jamison claims that the confessional memoir 'is often the opposite of solipsism: it creates dialogue. It elicits responses. It coaxes chorus like a brushfire' (qtd in Morrison 2019: np).

Paul

Memoirs take many forms. I recently wrote a crime novel (*A Time to Lie*) where I wrote out all my rejected crime stories into a crime novel about a failed crime writer. It became a memoir of my writing journey in a disguised from – the crime novel genre.

I began writing creatively because of a book on writing by David Bartholomy called *Sometimes even the President has to Stand Naked* (Bartholomy 1982). This book asks writers to be honest, expose themselves, write about intimacy and secrets, unmask, deconstruct, demystify, open wounds, let in the light. It is a memoir of a writing journey disguised as a textbook of writing the radical. This book, we hope, is a similar book that tells our story, and enables you to tell yours. We, you and us, we are all in the business of going naked. We allow our readers to get to know who we are, and as we do that, we also get to know ourselves in new ways.

EXERCISE: *Final naked freewrite*

Using the title 'The Root of Things', write without stopping for five minutes about the root of things – whatever that means to you. Don't worry about spelling or grammar, just go – experiment. Be poetic. Be random. No boundaries in form or content. Be angry. Be sad. Be joyful. Be impossible. Write as if no one will read this.

When you are done, read over what you've written. Is this piece to keep for yourself? Is it to burn? Is it a 'blob' or a lump of clay out of which something can be made in your memoir? Is it the ending to your collection of exercises, and the possibly the end of your radical memoir?

The decision is yours.

The beauty is that you have allowed yourself to go to the root of an aspect of you, to push the idea of memoir to the limit. You've taken risks.

What have you found?

Writing a radical memoir means getting to know who you are. The journey starts as an artist's journey, only as writers we don't have a canvas and paint. We don't have a piece of soapstone or rough marble. We don't have clay. Therefore we have to first make that. We have to fashion the 'clay' or stone out of the first principle of creation: imagination. First comes the picture of a story. Maybe the beginning falls into your head while you're in the shower. Then a middle or final image appears and you know these need to go in the imagined memoir somewhere. And then, the hardest part. Throwing down words. Making clay. Fashioning rough rock out of the firings of your own neurons. And then come words. You start somewhere. The words appear awkward, rough, misplaced. You build something that looks chaotic. At this point many people look at what they've 'wrought' in despair and think, I can't do this!

But that's just the beginning. This is the path to self-actualizing. As you write your life, your story, you shape yourself. You re-imagine yourself. You re-create the selves you have been and you become, not just the creator of that old self, but the progenitor of your new self – this writing being, who stands back and observes all your selves in action – as you write and narrate. This is a profound journey to awareness of self or selves – an awareness of you, past and present, an awareness of you as writer. The result is something necessary: humility. If you feel humbled, inadequate, raw, because the journey itself is fraught – but also because your words may feel for the most part inadequate – then know, please know, you are on the right path.

The journey is a constant becoming. As you write, you may question the validity of the memory; you may feel insecure about revealing the truth – and yet you still struggle on. You wrestle with words and sometimes you love them and much of the time you hate them for not being put together quite right, but the story is more powerful than your own ego, so you keep going. And here's the thing: after chiselling away, for months, maybe years even, throwing 'blobs' together, pushing them into shape as you would with clay, carving away as you would with stone, or wood, the question of *Who am I*, and *Why am I telling you this story*? begins to answer itself. Your collection of 'blobs' generated as you read and worked through the book could be the rough and precious material that you can shape into the book that you wanted to write.

Immortality

When you've written the memoir, or your portfolio of biographemes, or your autrebiography, whether it's in draft form or complete, you have become more you than you were before, because you've been on a journey. You have muscles where you thought there was no strength, you've found beautiful hidden treasures you didn't know existed – you've more than likely discovered a voice that you may not even recognize as your own. But also, you have left your mark on the sand, whether the memoir gets published or not. Others may see it. Or they may not. The tide may rush in and wash away your words, but the deeds that shaped them, the *you* that wrote them, remains.

I was here!

References

Anderson, L. 2011. *Autobiography*. Routledge, New York.

Attridge, D. 2004. *J. M. Coetzee and the Ethics of Reading*. The University of Chicago Press, Chicago.

Barthes, R. 1972. *Critical Essays*. R. Howard (trans.), Northwestern University Press, Evanston.

Barthes, R. 1975. *The Pleasure of the Text*. R. Miller (trans.), Hill and Wang, New York.

Barthes, R. 1977. *Roland Barthes by Roland Barthes*. R. Howard (trans.), Farrar, Straus and Giroux, New York.

Bartholomy, D. 1982. *Sometimes Even the President Has to Stand Naked*. Prentice Hall, New Jersey.

Baumeister, R. F. & L. S. Newman. 1994. 'How Stories Make Sense of Personal Experiences: Motives That Shape Autobiographical Narratives'. *Personality and Social Psychology Bulletin* 20, 6: 676–90

Beja, M. 1971. *Epiphany in the Modern Novel*. University of Washington Press, Seattle.

Benjamin, W. 2009 (1928). *One-way Street*. Penguin, Sydney.

Bruner, J. 1991. 'The Narrative Construction of Reality'. *Critical Inquiry* 18, 1 (Autumn): 1–21.

Campbell, J. 1949. *Hero with a Thousand Faces*. Pantheon Books, New York.

Campbell, J. 2004. *Pathways to Bliss: Mythology and Personal Transformation*. New World Library, New York.

Capote, T. 1966. *In Cold Blood*. Random House, New York.

Carrano, M. A. 2009. *Asleep in the Helix: Survival and the Science of Self-Realization*. Avatar Paradigms, North Haven, CT.

Chopin, K. 1894. 'The Dream of an Hour'. *Vogue*. December 6. Later reprinted in *St. Louis Life* (January 5, 1895) as 'The Story of an Hour'.

Cisneros, S. 1984. *The House on Mango Street*. Arte Público Press, Houston, TX.

Claire-Robson, E. 2011. *Collective Memoir as Public Pedagogy: A Study of Narrative, Writing, and Memory*. University of British Columbia Theses and Dissertations. https://open.library.ubc.ca/soa/cIRcle/collections/ubctheses/24/items/1.0055329. Accessed 08/03/2022.

Coetzee, J. M. 1992. *Doubling the Point: Essays and Interviews*. D. Attwell (ed.), Harvard University Press, Cambridge.

Coetzee, J. M. 1999. 'A Fiction of the Truth'. *Sydney Morning Herald* (27 November).

Coetzee, J. M. 1998. *Boyhood: Scenes from Provincial Life*. Penguin, London.

Codrescu, A. 1994. 'Adding to My Life', in K. Ashley, L. Gilmore & G. Peters (eds), *Autobiography & Postmodernism.* The University of Massachusetts Press, Amherst, 22–30.

Coullie, J. et al. 2006. *Selves in Question: Interviews on Southern African Auto/biography.* University of Hawai'i Press, Honolulu.

Couric, K. 2021. *Going There.* Little, Brown and Company, New York.

Cunxin, Li. 2003. *Mao's Last Dancer.* Penguin, London.

Davidow, S. 1992. *Freefalling.* Maskew-Miller Longman, Cape Town.

Davidow, S. 2007. *The Eye of the Moon.* Rainy Nights Press, Portland.

Davidow, S. 2008. *The Eye of the Moon.* Rainy Nights Press, Portland.

Davidow, S. 2016. *Whisperings in the Blood.* University of Queensland Press, Brisbane.

Davidow, S. 2018. *Shadow Sisters.* University of Queensland Press, Brisbane.

Davidow, S. & S. Khalil. 2022. *Runaways.* Ultimo Press, Sydney.

de Man, P. 1979. 'Autobiography as De-Facement'. *Modern Language Notes* 94: 919–30

Dementia Care Central. 2021. https://www.dementiacarecentral.com/caregiverinfo/brain-changes/. Accessed 04/03/2022.

Derrida, J. 1976. *Of Grammatology.* G. C. Spivak (trans.), Johns Hopkins University Press, Baltimore, MD.

Derrida, J. 1998. *The Ear of the Other: Otobiography, Transference, Translation: Texts and Discussions with Jacques Derrida.* P. Kamuf et al (trans.), University of Nebraska Press, Lincoln.

Didion, J. 1969. 'On Reading a Notebook', *Slouching towards Bethlehem.* Andre Deutsch, London. http://www.ranablog.com/pdfs/didion.pdf. Accessed 07/03/2022.

Didion, J. 1998. 'Last Words'. *The New Yorker.* October 25. https://www.newyorker.com/magazine/1998/11/09/last-words-6. Accessed 05/03/2022.

Dovey, C. & E. Bell. 2022. *Mothertongues.* Penguin Random House, Australia.

Drabble, M. 2010. 'Margaret Drabble', in S. Cline & C. Angier (eds), *The Arvon Book of Life Writing: Writing Biography, Autobiography and Memoir.* Methuen, York, 110–11.

Eggers, D. 2001. *A Heartbreaking Work of Staggering Genius.* Vintage, New York.

Federman, R. 2011. *Federman's Fictions: Innovation, Theory, and the Holocaust.* Jeffrey R. Di Leo (ed.), State University of New York Press, New York.

Fowles, J. 1992. *The French Lieutenant's Woman.* Penguin, London.

Freytag, G. 1863. *Die Technik des Dramas.* https://web.archive.org/web/20090116004731/http://www.matoni.de/technik/tec_inh.htm. Accessed 04/03/2022.

Furr, N. 2011. 'How Failure Taught Edison to Repeatedly Innovate'. *Forbes.* June 9. https://www.forbes.com/sites/nathanfurr/2011/06/09/how-failure-taught-edison-to-repeatedly-innovate/?sh=6fe16cc265e9. Accessed 10/03/2022.

Gilmore, L. 1994. *Autobiographics: A Feminist Theory of Women's Self-Representation.* Cornell University Press, Ithaca.

Gornick, V. 1996. 'Why Memoir Now?' *The Women's Review of Books* 13: 10/11.

Green, M. C. 2021. 'Transportation into Narrative Worlds', in L. B. Frank & P. Falzone (eds), *Entertainment-Education behind the Scenes.* Palgrave Macmillan, Cham. https://doi.org/10.1007/978-3-030-63614-2_6

Hale, C. 2012. 'Sentences Crisp, Sassy, Stirring'. *The New York Times.* May 28. https://opinionator.blogs.nytimes.com/2012/05/28/sentences-crisp-sassy-stirring/. Accessed 05/03/2022.

Hale, C. 2013. 'There's Parataxis, and Then There's Hypotaxis'. *The Chronicle of Higher Education*. August 7. https://web.archive.org/web/20150318060303/https://www.chronicle.com/blogs/linguafranca/2013/08/07/parataxis-and-hypotaxis/. Accessed 05/03/2022.

Hawkins, Falconer Al-Hindi, Moss & Kern. 2016. 'Practicing Collective Biography'. *Geography Compass* 10, 4 (April): 165–78.

Jacobs, J. U. 2011. '(N)either Afrikaner (n)or English: Cultural cross-over in J. M. Coetzee's Summertime'. *English Academy Review: Southern African Journal of English Studies* 28, 1: 39–52.

Jaworski, J. 1996. *Synchronicity: The Inner Path of Leadership*. Berrett-Kohler Publishing, Oakland.

Joyce, J. 1914. *The Dubliners*. Grant Richards Ltd., London.

Joyce, J. 1922. *Ulysses*. Shakespeare and Company, London.

Joyce, J. 2000 (1916). *A Portrait of the Artist as a Young Man*. Penguin, London.

Justin, N. 2021. 'Katie Couric's New Autobiography "Going There" Reads More Like a Vendetta Than a Memoir'. *Star Tribune*. October 25. https://www.startribune.com/katie-courics-new-autobiography-going-there-reads-more-like-a-vendetta-than-a-memoir/600109789/. Accessed 04/03/2022.

Kant, I. 2004. *Prolegomena to Any Future Metaphysics*. G. Hatfield (trans.), Cambridge University Press, Cambridge.

Keats, J. 1819. 'Ode on a Grecian Urn', first published anonymously in *Annals of the Fine Arts*. University of Michigan Press, Ann Arbor.

Kesey, K. 1962. *One Flew over the Cuckoo's Nest*. Viking, New York.

Kusek, R. 2012. 'Writing Oneself, Writing the Other: J. M. Coetzee's Fictional Autobiography in Boyhood, Youth and Summertime'. *Werkwinkel* 7, 1: 97–116.

Lacan, J. 2001. 'The Mirror Stage as Formative of the Function of the I as Revealed in Psychoanalytic Experience'. in V. B. Leitch et al (eds), *The Norton Anthology of Theory and Criticism*: W. W. Norton & Co, New York, 1285–90.

Larson, C. 1972. *The Emergence of African Fiction*. Indiana University Press, Indianapolis.

Lee, L. 2005. *Dialectics of the Body: Corporeality in the Philosophy of Theodor Adorno*. Routledge, New York.

Lejeune, P. 1977. 'Autobiography in the Third Person'. *New Literary History* 9, 1: Self-Confrontation and Social Vision (Autumn): 27–50.

Lejeune, P. 1982. 'The Autobiographical Contract', in T. Todorov (ed.), *French Literary Theory Today*. Cambridge University Press, Cambridge, 192–222.

Lejeune, P. 1982. 'The Autobiography of Those Who Do Not Write'. *On Autobiography*, 185–240.

Lejeune, P. 1989. 'The Autobiographical Pact', in *On Autobiography*. University of Minnesota Press, Minneapolis, 3–30.

MacDonald, H. 2014. *H Is for Hawk*. Jonathan Cape, London.

Madigan, S. 2011. *Narrative Therapy*. American Psychological Association.

Manathunga, C., A. L. Black & S. Davidow. 2020. *Walking towards a Valuable Academic Life. Discourse: Studies in the Cultural Politics of Education*. DOI: 10.1080/01596306.2020.1827222

Maslow, A. H. 1943. 'A Theory of Human Motivation'. *Psychological Review* 50, 4: 370–96.

Mater, H. 2016. *The Return*. Penguin, London.

McCann, C. 2020. *Apeirogon*. Bloomsbury, London.

Mehl-Madrona, L. 2015. *Remapping Your Mind: The Neuroscience of Self-Transformation through Story*. Bear & Company, New York.

Metacognition. https://harappa.education/harappa-diaries/what-is-metacognition/

Morrison, B. 2019. 'The Naked Truth: How to Write a Memoir'. *The Guardian*. 14 December. https://www.theguardian.com/books/2019/dec/14/the-naked-truth-how-to-write-a-memoir. Accessed 10/03/2022.

Murdock, M. 1982. 'Interview' with B. Lynn Goodwin, Maureen Murdock. http://www.maureenmurdock.com/emotionaltruth.html. Accessed 07/03/2022.

Mushakavanhu, T. 2011. 'White Rhodesia Was Not Africa: It was England in the Tropics'. *Mazwi* (30 October). http://www.mazwi.net/interviews/interview-white-rhodesia-was-not-africa-it-was-england-in-the-tropics. Accessed 04/03/2022.

Nabokov, V. 1951. *Speak, Memory!* Victor Gollancz, London.

Nabokov, V. 1990. *Strong Opinions*. Vintage, London.

Nordquist, R. 2019. 'Hypotaxis in English Sentences'. *Thought.Co*. 16 November https://www.thoughtco.com/hypotaxis-grammar-and-prose-style-1690948. Accessed 05/03/2022.

Olsen, K. 2013. *Boy, Lost*. University of Queensland Press, Brisbane.

O'Reilly, M. 2014. ' "Am I dying?" *The Honest Answer*', Ted Talks, July, https://www.ted.com/talks/matthew_o_reilly_am_i_dying_the_honest_answer/transcript?language=en). Accessed 27/02/2022.

O'Rourke, M. 2017. 'Instability in the Contemporary Memoir', in Bunty Avieson, Fiona Giles, Sue Joseph (eds), *Mediating Memory*. Routledge, London, 13–28

Pace, S. 2012. 'Writing the Self into Research: Using Grounded Theory Analytic Strategies in Autoethnography'. *TEXT* 16 (Special 13): 1–15. https://textjournal.scholasticahq.com/article/31147. Accessed 27/02/2022.

Painter, R. M. 2009. 'Healing Personal History: Memoirs of Trauma and Transcendence', in *Existence, Historical Fabulation, Destiny. Analecta Husserliana (The Yearbook of Phenomenological Research)*, vol 99. Springer, Dordrecht.

Pelzer, D. 1995. *A Child Called It*. Penguin, New York.

Proust, M. 1913–27. *A la recherche de temps perdu (In Search of Lost time)*. Grasset and Gallimard, Paris.

Pynchon, T. 1966. *The Crying of Lot 49*. J.B. Lippincott & Co., Philadelphia.

Rushdie, S. 1979. 'Calvino Holds Up a Mirror to Nature and Writes about the Mirror'. Salman Rushdie's blurb on the back of Calvino's *If on a Winter Night a Traveller*.

Sacks, O. 2007. *Musicophilia: Tales of Music and the Brain*. Knopf, New York.

Saunders, M. 2010. *Self Impression: Life-Writing, Autobiografiction, and the Forms of Modern Literature*. Oxford University Press, Oxford.

Scholes, R. 1969. 'Introduction', in *The Elements of Fiction*. Oxford University Press, Oxford.

Shelley, P. 1818. 'Ozymandias', first published in *The Examiner*, A Sunday Paper, on politics, domestic economy and theatricals, John Hunt, London.

Stumbrys, T., D. Erlacher, M. Schädlich & M. Schredl. 2012. 'Induction of Lucid Dreams: A Systematic Review of Evidence'. *Consciousness and Cognition* 21, 3: 1456–75. doi: 10.1016/j.concog.2012.07.003

Taddeo, L. 2019. *Three Women*. Simon and Schuster, New York.

Twain, M. 1884. *The Adventures of Huckleberry Finn*. Penguin, New York.

Updike, J. 1961. 'A&P'. *The New Yorker*. Accessed 02/08/2022.

Valentine, C. 2015. 'Marcel Proust's *In Search of Lost Time*'. *Huffington Post*. https://www. huffpost.com/entry/tldr-prousts-in-search-of-lost-time_n_559e8cb1e4b096729155 8d31. Accessed 28/02/2022.

Von Tirpitz, A. 1972. *My Memoirs: Recollections of a World War I German Grand Admiral*. Lucknow Books, New York.

Vonnegut, K. 1972. *Slaughterhouse 5*. Panther Books, St Albans.

Ward, T. 2014. *Esquire*. 23 July. https://www.esquire.com/uk/culture/news/a6742/ raymond-chandler-quotes/. Accessed 05/03/2022.

Whitman, W. 1982. *Complete Poetry and Collected Prose*. Justin Kaplan (ed.), The Library of America, New York.

Williams, P. 2008. *Soldier Blue*. New Africa Books, Cape Town.

Williams, P. 2013. 'There Is No Hereafter'. *Meanjin* 71, 4 (Summer): 178–82.

Williams, P. 2015. '31 Murdering Creek Road'. *Tincture Journal* 10, n.p.

Williams, P. 2019a. *Twelve Days*. Bloodhound Books, Cambridge.

Williams, P. 2019b. 'Autrebiography'. *TEXT* 23, 2.

Williams, P. 2020. *Novel Ideas: Writing Innovative Fiction*. Bloomsbury, London.

Williams, L. & Tammy. 2015. *Not Just Black and White*. Brisbane, UQP.

Wirick, R. 2006. *One Hundred Siberian Postcards*. Telegram Books, London.

Wright, A. 2015. *Tracker*. Giramondo, Sydney.

Index